The Gems She Wore

JAMES PLUNKETT

The Gems She Wore

A Book of Irish Places

HOLT, RINEHART AND WINSTON

New York   Chicago   San Francisco

Contents

To
Peadar O'Donnell

*Rich and rare were the gems she wore**
And a bright gold ring on her wand she bore
But, oh! her beauty was far beyond
Her sparkling gems and snow-white wand

'Lady! dost thou not fear to stray,
So lone and lovely, thro' this bleak way?
Are Erin's sons so good or so cold
As not to be tempted by woman or gold?'

'Sir Knight! I feel not the least alarm;
No son of Erin will offer me harm;
For, tho' they love woman and golden store,
Sir Knight they love honour and virtue more!'

On she went, and her maiden smile
In safety lighted her round the Green Isle;
And blest forever was she who relied
Upon Erin's honour and Erin's pride.

THOMAS MOORE (*Melodies*)

*'A young lady of great beauty, adorned with jewels and a costly dress, undertook a journey alone, from one end of the kingdom to the other, with a wand only in her hand, at the top of which was a ring of exceeding great value; and such an impression had the laws and government of this monarch (Brian) made on the minds of all the people, that no attempt was made upon her honour, nor was she robbed of her clothes or jewels'.

Warner's History of Ireland, Vol. 1, Book 10

7

Illustrations

Preface

BOOKS about tours (to adapt Wolfe Tone's remark) are made very much like apothecaries' mixtures—by pouring out of one vessel into another. What follows has been made on the same principle: by bringing together what was first gathered through travel in the company of those who were infinitely better informed or by reading what they had written; through more modest personal research undertaken as a background to radio and television programmes about Ireland over a number of years, or simply through everyday encounters and conversations. The most it can hope to do is to give the tourist, whether native or foreign, a sketch of Ireland through the eyes of someone who has valued simple information about personalities and events for the dimension it adds to one's understanding of people and their thinking, the meaning of landscape and the ordinary pleasures of travel and reflection.

I have refrained deliberately from any essay on the present situation in the Six Counties. There are many informed books devoted to it alone, by men whose authority is based on scholarship or direct experience or both, neither of which I can claim. If I have tuppence worth to add in a personal way, it is that I do not believe history is the culprit or that Plantation is to blame. Extensive areas in the Republic, also subjected to Plantation, have not had to suffer the same ordeal of sectarian bigotry. In the North the growing together of different cultures which is the normal process of history was inhibited deliberately by those who found it profitable to divide and rule and who, now that the manufactured situation is out of control, will only exist as long as they can lead England by the nose. When that fails Ireland may begin to hope for unity and, ultimately, for peace, though through what initiatives of reconciliation God alone, at present, knows. I have a friend who is convinced the first effective step would be a *Ban The Bible* campaign.

As for the rest, although there may be little or nothing in what follows that is new to the well-informed, others like myself who, to keep the memory topped-up, have to keep drawing from the well, may find it of interest. There is no claim whatever to scholarship, but there is engagement and, I hope, a regard for those associations of place which can move rewardingly the imagination and the heart.

JAMES PLUNKETT

Acknowledgements

QUOTATIONS IN THE TEXT

The author and the publishers wish to make the following acknowledgements: For permission to reproduce the poem on page 20 beginning 'Ringletted Youth of my Love' by Douglas Hyde, thanks are due to the Dr Douglas Hyde Trust. Messrs Curtis Brown Ltd kindly allowed us to print the passage from Sean O'Faolain's book, *The Irish*, appearing on page 23, and Constable and Company Ltd allowed reproduction of Oliver St. John Gogarty's poem 'Ringsend' on page 27. We are grateful to The Bodley Head for their permission to print the opening lines of *Ulysses* by James Joyce (page 39) and to Jonathan Cape Ltd for the passage on page 44 from *Portrait of the Artist as a Young Man* by the same author. Thanks are due to Faber & Faber Ltd for allowing reproduction of lines by Louis MacNeice from the poem 'Dublin' (pages 42 and 122). MacGibbon & Kee kindly gave permission to quote from works by Patrick Kavanagh: lines from the essay entitled 'From Monaghan to the Grand Canal' on page 51 and the poem 'Lines written on a Seat on the Grand Canal, Dublin' on page 51. Lines from the poems 'September 1913' and 'Three Songs to the One Burden' on pages 62 and 167 and from *Autobiographies* on page 167 and the poem 'In Memory of Eva Gore-Booth and Countess Markiewicz' on page 174, all by W. B. Yeats, are reprinted by permission of M. B. Yeats and the Macmillan Companies. We are grateful to the Dolmen Press for allowing us to reproduce extracts from

Acknowledgements

The *Autobiography of James Clarence Mangan*, edited by James Kilroy, on page 63, and from Peadar O'Donnell's *There will be Another Day* on page 193. Simon Campbell kindly allowed us to include poems by Joseph Campbell appearing on pages 75–79: 'The Spanish Lady', 'Earth of Cualann', 'The Chimney Sweep' and 'The Osiers Sellers', and Allen Figgis gave permission to quote from Austin Clarke's preface to *Poems of Joseph Campbell* (page 89). The extract on page 103 from *Old Ireland, her Scribes and Scholars* by Robert E. McNally, S. J. is reprinted by permission of the publishers, Gill & Macmillan Ltd, Dublin. Frank O'Connor's poem 'The Hermitage' (page 108) is reprinted by permission of A.D. Peters and Company. John Murray Ltd. kindly allowed us to quote from John Betjeman's poem 'Sunday in Ireland' on page 125. Finally, thanks are due to Methuen & Company Ltd. who gave permission to reproduce an extract from E. Curtis' book *A History of Ireland* which appears on page 144.

PHOTOGRAPHS

The photographs on pages 52 and 173 and the aerial photograph of O'Connell Street, Dublin on page 33 are by Edward Mirzoeff. (The Dublin photograph is used by kind permission of BBC TV.) The photograph on pages 130–31 is by David Mansell. The photograph of Sean O'Casey's room is by Dermot Goulding. The montage on page 85 is comprised of photographs by David Mansell and Dermot Goulding. 'Race Card Seller' by Jack B. Yeats is reproduced by kind permission of The Commissioners of Public Works in Ireland. The photograph on page 192 is by T. Hayde. The photograph on page 188 appears by permission of The Illustrated London News. Thanks are due to Patrick King for the illustration on page 17. The photographs on page 81 are by Brian Perman. Prints of the photographs which appear on pages 60, 95 and 153 were kindly authorised by Radio Telefís Éireann. The photograph of W. B. Yeats in Cap Martin is by Nora G. Heald. The photographs on pages 66, 72, 87, 98, 103, 126, 128, 137, 140, 155, 158, 164, 169, 175 and 201 all appear by kind permission of Board Fáilte Éireann.

I

Myth and Reality

S AMUEL BECKETT tells a story in which the nations are
asked to write an essay on The Camel. The Frenchman's
was called 'The Camel and Love'; the German's was 'The
Camel and Metaphysics'; the Irishman's 'The Camel and the
fight for Irish Freedom'. Frank O'Connor has noted that books
which begin with a summary of Irish history tend to remain
unread. Both are warnings to be borne in mind. On the other
hand, history is not utterly dispensable. Nations are as much
their own past as what they eat and drink; people are shaped by
what has moved their poets to poetry and their musicians to
music. They have, in addition, incurable habits of imagination
and remembrance and with these they transform their natural
surroundings. However beautiful virgin land may be, it only
pleases the eye. Land that has cradled and served a people can
do more. It breathes back something of that mysterious pageant
and can stir the depths of the heart. Patriots, certainly, are
capable of being unconscionable bores, as anyone who has had
to suffer them knows. Yet reflective and sensible men will
acknowledge that to achieve a sense of Place and Past, to be at
one (so to speak) with Before and After, is essential to man's
contentment, his pursuit of wholeness. Ceremony and tradition
are his meat and drink. It is now probably time for a legend.

Once upon a time, thousands of years ago, when the
country was inhabited by a race of wizards and sorcerers, the

three kings who ruled there were married to three sisters. Each of the sisters was beautiful and each in turn gave her name to the country. One of these sisters was called Banba, another Fodhla and the third, Eire. And it was from Eire Ireland got her name. Or so we were taught in school. It was a legend full of difficult, scholarly names, like 'Milesian' and 'Tuatha de Danaan' and it lit the imagination with an odd, bronze glow. It was only one of many stories given to us in the classrooms of the early thirties by teachers whose fierce nationalism was already becoming irrelevant. These teachers deserve exploration.

By the beginning of the nineteenth century the British conquest of Ireland looked at last like being complete. The Irish language had lost its place as a living tongue, Irish culture had gone underground, the poets and writers either turned to England for literary models or made do with a Stage Irishry which was as far from the realities as a strip cartoon (one has only to read Lover). It was as though Ireland, despairing of equality, was content to become the Empire's favourite buffoon. But within fifty years the situation was reversed by a new National movement involving the poets of the Young Ireland party and their paper The Nation. They were better propagandists than poets. The poetry in many cases was so bad that even John O'Leary, the Fenian leader and unbending Nationalist, found himself compelled to protest against what he termed 'the assumed right of patriots to perpetrate bad verses'. The propaganda, however, worked. The harp, the shamrock, the ancient kings and the Round Towers of Other Days became symbols of Irish Identity. Hitherto they had been part of the furniture, so to speak; now they were sacred remnants of a golden age, God's covenant with the Irish race. The trouble was they acquired as time went on, despite their antiquity, a Victorian aura. They were soon decorating the chocolate boxes.

Nevertheless, it was not all sentimentality. Scholars were rediscovering the riches of Gaelic civilization through the study of its monuments and its literature, while later in the century the founding of the Gaelic League began the long (and so far unsuccessful) struggle to restore the Irish language as the everyday speech of the country. Nationalism reached its full

It was as though Ireland, despairing of equality, was content to become the Empire's favourite buffoon.

flowering in the Rising of 1916 and, after a period of bitter guerrilla warfare, in the setting up of the Irish Free State in 1922. The Peace terms, however, negotiated with Lloyd George, fell short of full freedom by sundering six of the Northern counties from the rest of Ireland, a situation which gave rise to civil war in the South between those who wanted the whole of Ireland free of British control and those who, although they wanted it too, felt it to be impossible either to negotiate or to achieve by force and decided that free Ireland, for the moment, would consist of the 26 Southern counties. To-day, over 50 years later, the British are still in the North and getting little good of it. If they could find some workable way of disentangling themselves, one feels, they would get out.

The relevant point is that all this was of very recent memory to the teachers I came up against in those chalky and often over-crowded classrooms of the thirties. They were all Irish speakers, some of them native speakers, and many of them had carried guns themselves during the guerrilla years—called 'The Troubles' in Ireland, where there is a tendency to think that if you refuse an evil its true name, it will go away. (The period 1939–1945, for instance, was referred to throughout as 'The Emergency'.)

As a result, although by and large they were good men, they were intoxicated with patriotism and intensely concerned to eradicate any remnants of servility or British influence from the young minds of the new State committed to their charge. To them, we ten and twelve year olds were the children of promise. I remember one of them, a mountain of a man who used to bang the desk with great hairy fists as he recited the foul deeds of the Sassenach:

Did they dare, did they dare to slay Eoghan Roe O'Neill?
Yes they slew with poison him they feared to meet with steel
May God wither up their hearts, may their blood cease to flow
May they walk in living death, who poisoned Eoghan Roe.

To be children of promise could be very terrifying, especially as the image of Ireland they were giving us bore no relationship to the world most of us were doing our best to grow up in.

There was another poem, much favoured, in which a highborn lady dressed in precious jewels goes unattended through the length and breadth of Ireland, perfectly confident that she will be unmolested.

> Sir Knight! I feel not the least alarm;
> No son of Erin will offer me harm;
> For, tho' they love woman and golden store,
> Sir Knight they love honour and virtue more.

Though tender of age, and too docile to say so, we were all realists enough to know that this was all bloody nonsense. Alternatively, if in some golden age the Irish were as blinded by Honour and Virtue as they would have us believe, then no wonder the Danes and the Normans and the English anticipated an easy passage when it came to taking our country from us. And as for the Gael's purity of mind and heart, if the evidence of the everyday speech of our neighbours was not sufficient (the patriots would explain that the English tongue had debased them) I personally had a grandfather who spoke Irish and had the habit when he had a few drinks taken of giving out verses in that language which I knew, from my poor grandmother's agitation, would not be fit for my childish ears had I understood them, though they probably did more than all the exhortations of the teachers to inspire interest in the language. That traditional Irish culture could be warm, and even bawdy as well as God-fearing—in a word, human—was not so much a carefully guarded secret as a fact the Honour and Virtue school steadfastly refused to recognise.

The poets of The Nation and their later imitators, although in style and form they followed the English rather than the Celtic tradition, were all in all to the ultra Patriots because of their political aims and the correctness of their morals, while very beautiful poems, unmistakably and refreshingly of the true Irish tradition, were never referred to, because they had a dangerous sense of life as well as of race. Scholars such as Douglas Hyde, for instance, let the cat out of the bag from time to time by translating Irish love songs which embarrassed official Ireland because there was a hint of hot blood about them.

The Gems She Wore

Ringletted youth of my love,
With thy locks bound loosely behind thee
You passed by the road above
But you never came in to find me;
Where was the harm for you
If you came for a little to see me;
Your kiss is a wakening dew
Were I ever so ill or so dreamy.

If I had golden store
I would make a nice little boreen
To lead straight up to his door
The door of the house of my storeen;
Hoping to God not to miss
The sound of his footfall in it,
I have waited so long for his kiss
That for days I have slept not a minute.

I thought, O my love! you were so—
As the moon is, or sun on a fountain,
And I thought after that you were snow,
The cold snow on top of the mountain;
And I thought after that you were more
Like God's lamp shining to find me
Or the bright star of knowledge before,
And the star of knowledge behind me.

You promised me high heeled shoes,
And satin and silk, my storeen
And to follow me, never to lose,
Though the ocean were round us roaring;
Like a bush in a gap in a wall
I am now left lonely without thee
And this house, I grow dead of, is all
That I see around or about me.

No highborn maiden there, prating of such abstractions as

'. . . to follow me, never to lose, though the ocean were round us roaring . . .'

Honour and Virtue, but a girl aching and tender for the sweet comforts of the flesh.

While Round Towers and Wrap-the-green-Flaggery ran riot in the classroom, an even stranger thing was happening in the world of politics. The country's leaders, their work of revolution completed, were reacting into conservative policies and an extraordinarily obsessive obscurantism. There was a striking outbreak of public piety, which the Church naturally encouraged. Ex-revolutionaries, who defied formal religion and had been forbidden the Sacraments at one time because of their unconstitutional activities, were now pillars of both Church and State. The new middle class of the thirties sternly supported them. Among the many public pruderies, literary censorship was the most notorious. In the opening years of the century J. M. Synge had earned the condemnation of the ultra patriots by writing a play (*In The Shadow of The Glen*) in which a young woman is suspected of being unfaithful to her elderly husband and eventually leaves him to walk the roads with a tramp who has nothing to offer except imagination and fine talk. This was regarded as an unforgivable slur on Irish womanhood. Later on Synge caused riots at The Abbey Theatre when one of his characters used the word 'shift' on the stage, reference to a female undergarment being regarded as completely unpermissible in mixed company. That was in the first decade of the twentieth century while the British were still here and such susceptibility might have been understandable. But in the 30s when the British had left, the same exaggerated sensitivity remained, so that the dramatist Sean O'Casey became the target of nationalistic abuse and further riots marked the production of his plays, though the ordinary Dublin people, as always, demonstrated their sanity and good taste by packing out the theatre for O'Casey performances.

What began with the setting up of the new State continued into the Forties. Some examples of current attitudes are to hand:

'A lot has been made lately of the banning of a fine novel because of one objectionable line. But it could be asked— why was that line there?'

The Leader 11/3/1942

'Children leaving school, for instance, should immediately be enrolled automatically in an organisation like the Gaelic League and they should be compelled to attend lectures (*on the Irish language*) at least twice a week.'

The Standard July 1943

'Superintendent Heron said that while not opposing the application in regard to men (for a drink licence extension during a dance at Balbriggan) he suggested that no drink should be served to women in the hotel during the dance. . . .

'The Justice said that he was altogether opposed to the principle of the objection, which interfered with human liberty. However, he would grant the application in this case,

and would order that the consumption of drink in the hotel during the exemption period should be confined to males.'
Evening Herald Sept. 1943

'Neither are there any dirty passages interlarded as bait for prurient readers, a trick which has become common with Anglo-Irish novelists who glory in realism.'
The Irish Book Lover May 1943

'It is one of the injustices of modern society that a wretched degenerate caught by the police in the commission of an indecent action is sentenced to punishment of great severity, whereas a George Moore or an Andre Gide walks the streets a free man and makes a fortune out of his crimes. As though a crook should be acquitted because his bit of burglary or swindling was a stroke of genius. Your seller of indecent postcards gets six months, and your immoral novelist gets the Prix Goncourt or something of the kind—in the sacred name of literature.'
Libraries & Literature from a Catholic Standpoint

When Revolutionaries attain power, the last thing they want is any continuation of war's irresponsibility. In their need to create a new respectability and conformity they over-react. All this is understandable but it can be hard to live with. In the thirties and forties Irish society reflected Religious Authoritarianism, prudery and a false mode of patriotic expression which sentimentalised history and its symbols out of all truth. The first to suffer were the writers, most of whom had themselves taken an active part in the struggle against oppression. They rejected the image of itself Irish Society was being given and in turn were harried by officialdom and abhorred by the new middle class—which found reassurance in the official image, and was described by Sean O'Faolain as representing:

'Defeatism in politics, laissez faire in social reform, a hypocritical pietism in religion . . . a class which breeds censorship, lay priests and arid traditionalism'.

The true heritage of national and religious culture was lost in half-truths and phoniness. If the situation has now been retrieved, it is due to the writers, the scholars and the general liberalising of Thought which began in Ireland as late as the middle fifties.

The world I myself grew up in was far removed from the ultra patriotic humours of classroom and public authority, though it too had its manifestations. Public houses, in particular, favoured Round Towers and shamrocks in plaster relief; I remember one such piece which showed a virtuous and honour-conscious female bent in grief above a musical instrument and a scroll underneath with the information 'Erin weeps over her stringless Harp'. And in my grandmother's house Robert Emmet's speech from the Dock hung side by side with my uncle's medals for service to King and Empire during the first World War, a juxtaposition which showed the good sense of that humble locality, which recognised that culture is a totality in which contradictions are harmonised.

Religion was a different matter. You could think disrespect-fully of a Round Tower or a Stringless Harp without any lasting repercussions. God could hit back. His speech for the souls who died in His displeasure was already available in the Penny Catechism and left no room for doubt. 'Depart from Me, ye cursed, into everlasting flames which were prepared for the Devil and his Angels'.

So Religion—I mean the Catholic religion—kept our young minds focussed on our essential depravity. At an early age we could distinguish between Attrition and Contrition; we knew the difference between Actual and Sanctifying Grace. It taught us how to confess our sins. We were experts on Sin: original sin, venial sin, mortal sin, sins of omission and commission, occasions of sin. There were reserved sins too, but these were for some obscure villainies. We were taught how to dissect sin in an examination of conscience; the gravity of the sin, its frequency, the amount of pleasure taken in it, was it deliberate or involuntary, had you gone into the occasion of sin. We were all little anatomists, trained to subject sin and its by-products to endless analysis. When all was parsed and analysed and ready for inspection, the slide clicked open and the soul was laid bare. Then the priest gave absolution. His hands held the keys to heaven and hell.

The Church had excommunicated the Fenians, it had condemned practically everything I later came to regard as worthwhile, yet for mature men of my childhood, even those who had suffered grievously from its intolerance, it guarded a Truth which was better than the sum of all its wrongheadedness. And so it came about with me. The Ireland I grew up in and its people found it as natural to believe in God as it was to breathe the air. This is partly a matter of history but, more so, an inherited disposition of race, with the same belief in the efficacy of austerity and personal prayer that informed the early Irish monks. No one stood up to his neck in freezing water any longer or set sail in a currach in search of the Land of the Blest, but many pilgrimaged annually to climb Patrick's Holy Mountain in penance for their sins and the sins of the world. Old people still fasted and drank black tea in the season of Lent. And one man, at least, Matt Talbot, a Dublin docker, slept on a board and wore chains under his clothes, so tightly wound about his body that they were discovered after his death to have bitten deeply into the flesh. Many thought him a bit cracked, of course: many more went to pray outside the door of his lodgings in Granby Lane. I remember the little improvised altar with its flowers and statues that stood on the window ledge before the tottering old house was pulled down. This was natural piety, as far removed from Religious formalism as were the ultra Patriots from the real thing.

2

The house I was born in stood by the sea, near to where the river Liffey enters Dublin Bay and halfway between the township of Ringsend and the suburbs of Sandymount.

Sandymount was respectable. It had houses with gardens breathing the sea air; quiet, hedge-lined walks; a Martello Tower which Mr. Pitt had had put there to keep a weather eye open for any sudden move of Napoleon (the one James Joyce

Sandymount Martello . . . *a Martello tower which Mr. Pitt had put there to keep a weather eye open for any sudden move of Napoleon, (the one James Joyce and Oliver St. John Gogarty had occupied was a few miles further on).*

and Oliver St. John Gogarty had occupied was a few miles further on), and a great golden sweep of strand to lift even a child's heart with views of Howth and the wide bay and the Dublin and Wicklow mountains.

Ringsend, by contrast, was poor. It had pawnshops, fish and chip shops, a soccer football ground, tenements, public houses and a leaning towards Saturday night shindies and continuous under-employment, despite its fishing boats, its gas works, its

Bottle House, Boland's Mill, the Hammond Lane Foundry and the Central Depot of the Dublin United Tramway Company.

Ringsend swarmed with dockers and boatmen, carters and labourers, many of whom worked only casually and some not at all. It was mad about soccer football and trade unionism, and although it could mount as fervent and impressive a Corpus Christi procession as the next, it knew enough about the doctrine of the Fall of Man to accept the daily practicalities of Good and Evil. Oliver St. John Gogarty wrote about it with affection:

RINGSEND
(After reading Tolstoi)

I will live in Ringsend
With a red-headed whore
And the fanlight gone in
Where it lights the halldoor;
And listen each night
For her querulous shout
As at last she streels in
And the pubs empty out.
To soothe that wild breast
With my old-fangled songs
Till she feels it redressed
From inordinate wrongs,
Imagined, outrageous
Preposterous wrongs,
Till peace at last comes
Shall be all I will do,
Where the little lamp blooms
Like a rose in the Stew;
And up the back garden
The sound comes to me
Of the lapsing, unsoilable
Whispering sea.

Sandymount, by the edge of the same lapsing and unsoilable sea, had only one black mark against it. It was the birthplace of the poet W. B. Yeats, who spoke in the Irish Senate in favour of divorce. Apart from that it seemed to be populated almost entirely by schools of equestrian young ladies who used the great strand for exercise at ebbtide. The strand was wide and beautiful, an expanse of sand with glistening pools, an expanse of sky with patterned clouds. On its way southwards the Strand Road led to Blackrock and Kingstown, a progress towards even greater glories of pride and respectability. But the road north through Ringsend reversed the procedure, exploring Thorncastle Street and Brunswick Street with their adjoining tenements, warrens of disease and hunger.

These were the two faces physical Dublin wore in my early childhood. It all seemed to depend on whether you turned left or right when you came out the halldoor.

If official Patriotism in those days showed no sign whatever of social conscience, Religion was trying to wake up. It had condemned Larkin and his followers in the gigantic labour upheaval of 1913, when a general strike paralysed Dublin for almost 8 months. Caught in the employment dilemma of the thirties, beset by Socialism and Communism, it became concerned in its turn about the children of promise and decided to arm us for the struggle against leftist theory (also condemned) through a school text book based on the Social Encyclical of Leo XIII (issued as far back as 1891) called, I think, A Manual of Catholic Social Science, which discussed the morality of strikes and had got so far along the road of progressive thinking as to propagate a Just Day's pay for a Just Day's work. It was unable to advance any more workable definition of what a just day's pay might be than that in general terms it should be sufficient to keep a labourer and his family in frugal comfort.

And what then, was frugal comfort? And suppose there was no day's work to be had—just or otherwise—for which a just day's pay ought to be paid? The Government, we were told, should encourage private enterprise. On no account, however, was it to go into competition with it. It appeared that the Law of God countenanced Private Enterprise only. It also appeared that the same immutable Law of God was strictly against State medicine, State Welfare, State Insurance, State run Schools,

Oliver St. John Gogarty *wrote about Ringsend with affection.*

State anything except State endowment of the private Corporation. The Manual defined Socialism and Communism for us, just in case we got led into damnation, for both Socialism and Communism were Mortal Sins. When the war in Spain began, I remember, it was General Franco who represented the law of God.

At the age of fourteen we took all this very seriously and felt ourselves well equipped, like good soldiers of Christ, to argue any dialectical materialist into a cocked hat, so that when I left school around the age of 17 to wander the streets, taking notice of things on my own account and scribbling little verses about what I saw, I received a great shock. When I read the verses over, I found myself, quite unexpectedly, on the side of the Godless.

> I must not be a Socialist
> Despite the sufferings
> Of hunger and privation
> And such unpleasant things
>
> For if I am a Socialist
> The theologians tell
> I'll suffer here and when I die
> I'll suffer down in hell
>
> God, much beset, approves the points
> The theologian raises
> But when we die I wonder who'll
> Be told to go to blazes?

These and numerous other deplorable little verses were as pitted with propaganda as anything that had ever appeared in The Nation, but they were a mile away from the thinking in the Manual of Catholic Social Science. Which shows, I suppose, that bad arguments do not have to be defeated by good ones. The years soon lead the young polemicist by the nose and the repetitions of experience rub the bad arguments away. I had no theories. I simply listened with the rest of the Sunday crowd to the men who shouted outside the City Hall and Foster Place.

Hear, hear, sang my heart. A patriot who saw Ireland in terms of her people was refreshing.

These ill-dressed orators, Larkin among them, ignored Social Science. They even ignored God. They were, by all respectable standards, outrageous. Yet they were undeniably Irish, as Irish as Robert Emmet or Wolfe Tone. And they had the habit of quoting James Connolly, one of the executed leaders of 1916:

'Ireland, as distinct from her people, is nothing to me; and the man who is bubbling over with love and enthusiasm for "Ireland", and can yet pass unmoved through our streets and witness all the wrong and the suffering, the shame and the degradation wrought upon the people of Ireland—yea, wrought by Irishmen upon Irish men and women, without burning to end it is, in my opinion, a fraud and a liar in his heart, no matter how he loves that combination of chemical elements he is pleased to call Ireland.'

Hear, hear, sang my heart. A patriot who saw Ireland in terms of her people was new and refreshing. It remained to be discovered that most sensible patriots had; that the ancient kings and queens, the saints and the monks, the scribes and the poets, were not inventions of the illustrators of old books and school histories, but people. The Great O'Neill, fleeing to Rome after the defeat at Kinsale, was a person—a very great person; the croppies of 1798 were young men with an interest in drink and sports, who died nevertheless, not for some maudlin Personification of Mother Ireland, but for a dream of liberty, equality and fraternity that had come from the Continent to goad the spirit into a hopeless onslaught on tyranny. Human hands had raised the Round Towers for protection against murderous enemies; the wolfhound was a hardy hunter, not a piece of decoration; the harp served human need when joy demanded a dance, or grief a lament, or God a hymn, or love its celebration or consolation. Carolan, the most celebrated of travelling harpers and one of the last, was fond of the bottle and knew it. But when his friends urged sobriety he had his answer ready for them.

'He who would give up drink', he said, waving them aside, 'is a foolish person'.

So is he who would give up flesh and blood ancestors— never mind their sins and their shortcomings—in exchange for cardboard idealisations.

When the middle class lie of my youth was nailed at last, it was the turn of the writers and the poets. They had better things by far to say. They understood that a country is its people and that landscape which has soaked in the sweat and blood of the living acquires a natural sanctity. Its monuments too, and its carved stones, are endowed with life and speak with tongues.

Sean O'Casey's room (opposite above). *This is not the actual room but a reconstruction made for a film set. Incidentally, the Catholic statue and holy pictures puzzled me (O'Casey was a Protestant) until I remembered that he shared the room with a Catholic pal (who was later upset to find himself paraded publicly as Seamus Shields in* The Shadow of a Gunman*).*

O'Connell Street, Dublin (opposite below) *from the air.*

Molly Malone

THE Bovril sign overlooked College Green and the old houses of Parliament and was a great wonder. Whenever our Sunday visit to my grandmother left us belated, with the last tram gone to its shed in Ringsend or Donnybrook or Clontarf, my mother would push the pram home through dark and deserted streets and I would drag myself along beside her, half asleep, my hand holding one corner of it for support, our footsteps sounding far away, as though they were not ours at all. My younger sister slept peacefully in the pram and for the most part I let my eyes remain closed and left it to my nose to tell me where we were. The smells at that late hour were the best landmarks: the breath of shuttered public houses, the Dodder smell at Ringsend Bridge, the smell of baking bread at Boland's Mills, the coal tar smell at the Gas Works, the horse smells from the deserted cab rank at Westland Row Station. At Tara Street the clock on the tower wore a face like the moon in the dark air above the houses and I would open my eyes to read the words 'Fire Station' on the red sign on the building underneath it. In summer dried horse dung strewed the gutter in a fine powder like sawdust and covered the debris of the day—spent matches, discarded fruit peelings, empty cigarette cartons. That had its smell too. Then, passing the Crampton monument in D'Olier Street we turned the corner in College Green and the Bovril sign jerked one awake.

High up above Trinity College and the sleeping buildings it made a firework display against the night sky. The huge letters lit up, went out; lit up again in a different colour, changed colour again, changed once more, then began to mix the colours in criss-cross patterns and movements that seemed inexhaustible in their variety. My mother stopped to look and my friends the statues looked too; Tom Moore at College Green eternally polishing up a poem, Burke and Goldsmith outside Trinity College, Henry Grattan opposite the Bank of Ireland, his hand held up to arrest your attention. The only outsider was King Billy. He sat on his horse further down the street, turning its orange rump and his own on everybody, and would have nothing to do with it.

I was seven or eight at the time (it was the nineteen twenties) and something of an expert on statues. O'Connell, on O'Connell Bridge, was the Liberator who had won Catholic Emancipation in 1829. He had angels about him with bullet holes in their enormous breasts. Grattan had spoken against the Act of Union with Britain in 1800. Moore was the poet whose songs my aunt sang at Sunday musical evenings. King Billy had won the battle of the Boyne for the Protestants. Protestants, generally speaking, were God-save-the-Kingers and went to Mass in the afternoon or the night instead of in the morning. All their male children had sharp noses and were members of the Boys' Brigade. They ate meat on Fridays.

This was information gleaned from friends of my own age or from my father, who himself was in an ambiguous position, for he had fought all through the world war and had medals at home, the stubbed butt of a cigarette given to him by the then Prince of Wales on some battlefield or other and an enormous album of wartime photographs to prove it. He paraded on Remembrance Day with his comrades. I remember seeing him march to the temporary Cenotaph at Stephen's Green and women weeping as they looked on. It was, even at that age, an intensely moving experience. The bugles played the Last Post, the crowd observed the one minute's silence, though it was frequently interrupted by shouts from extremists who spent the rest of the day snatching poppies from the coats of people who were honouring their slaughtered husbands and sons. My father had lost one of his brothers and many a childhood friend in the war, and it is a measure of Dublin's tragic dissensions at that time that it required guts and a willingness to suffer insult and injury to mourn them publicly. To his way of thinking, he had fought, not for King and country, but for what he called 'little Belgium and the freedom of small nations'. (My mother, who was inclined that way, used the phrase 'little *Catholic* Belgium'.) He detested King Billy, the Masonic Order and the enemies of Irish independence. He personified a paradox which for years caused tragic and quite unnecessary divisions. In those years he was still a young man with a romantic passion for war films. I suppose, after his experience of the reality, it was a great luxury to be able to consider it all from the comfort of an upholstered seat. He brought me with him to such things as 'O'Reilly V.C.' at the Corinthian. Sound films had not yet been developed and a pit orchestra provided the music and effects. The one in the Corinthian had a 'cellist who, I discovered years later, knew James Joyce and couldn't stand him.

They were difficult days, with much unemployment, a great war just finished which had bereaved many a Dublin family, and a national Rising and Civil War which had brought the same tragedy to many more. 'Great hatred, little room' (as Yeats said) 'maimed us at the start'.

It was easy enough for me to stand and marvel at the bullet marks in O'Connell's angels, but for my parents the memory of Dublin in flames was a recent one; it had happened only in 1916, when the rebels against British rule occupied the General Post Office in O'Connell Street and ran up the tricolour above Dublin's principal street. By some miracle of grace, after 700 years of failure, it remained there and the city, at last, became ours. But the Black and Tan war and the civil war which followed it had kept the city in a constant state of anguish, so that even in the middle twenties, when it was all officially over, the streets still bore the grey look of suffering. There were still intermittent outbreaks of violence as men who had grown used to guns and simple solutions paid off old scores.

I remember what was probably the last of them. I was

36

standing one Sunday evening with my grandfather at the door of his house looking at a magnificent sunset which filled the sky above the spire of Ringsend Church, when the street was galvanised with cries of 'Stop Press'. Doors opened and the news was shouted from one neighbour to another. Kevin O'Higgins, the Minister for Justice, had been shot dead that morning on his way to Mass. That was on 10th July 1927. The sense of shock froze people and listening houses into an ineradicable memory.

There were less harrowing incidents, including the snatching of Union Jacks (they shouldn't have been there anyway) from outside loyal institutions which refused to recognise that the old glory had departed. There were attacks on statues. Someone tried to saw the head off George II in St. Stephen's Green; King Billy at College Green was blown up by a landmine, much to the satisfaction of nearly everyone. It was the end of a long and troubled career. From 1701, when it was first erected, William III's statue had been the target of attack. When the Williamites decked it with flags, the Jacobites came along after them and tarred and feathered it. The students of Trinity stole its sword and truncheon because, they said, it was by way of meditated insult that it had turned its rump to the gateway of their hallowed institution. It was frequently daubed with mud and often enough the early morning citizens found a second rider, made of straw, sitting behind the king. Even after the attack in 1929, when a weary Corporation had it moved to one of its yards out of public view, it was still followed relentlessly. One morning a watchman found somebody had sawn off the king's head. That finished William III so far as College Green was concerned.

Yet despite its tensions and its tragedies, Dublin was a good city to grow up in. The sea was at its feet, its Georgian buildings gave it nobility, its squares and its expanses of water made it a place of openness and light and air. Water especially. You could see great expanses of sky above you which were reflected for double measure at your feet. The Grand Canal with its trees, its still stretches of reed bordered water, its locks with their silver cascades, was a place of peace where the adult walked in the evening and the young fished for tiddlers with net and jamjar.

In summer it was a swimming pool free of charge. There was the Dodder river too, which you could walk beside from Ringsend to Rathfarnham. The Liffey, looking westwards from O'Connell Bridge, presented supreme sunsets against which the houses along its banks and its sequence of bridges were smoky silhouettes. And of course, the sea. It began almost at the heart of the city, wandered by Ringsend Park and stretched past the cottages at Irishtown, the Martello tower at Sandymount, the village of Blackrock. When the tide was fully out there was level sand for miles with pools and lakes to reflect the sky, and the blue outline of Howth hill with its yellow gorse bushes floating in the distance. The train ran along its border from Westland Row Station to Bray in County Wicklow, a journey made by hundreds of poor city mothers and children during the summer, most of them to Merrion Gates: a few who had probably saved for a special treat, went further to listen to the band on the esplanade at Bray or climb the steep paths of the Head. They were always armed with teapots, kettles, cups, parcels of sandwiches, towels and bathing togs. Their picnic fires added the smell of wood smoke to the salt air, the children bathed or built sand castles and collected shells. In the evening the trams and the trains brought them back to the city streets again, often enough to grinding poverty and airless tenements, where memories of sea and sand made it easier for mothers and filled the dreams of sleeping children.

The road along the front at Sandymount is high above strand level and the sea wall low enough to leave the wide sweep of the bay completely open. It is still a pleasant place to walk despite the worst efforts of the Port and Docks Board and the E.S.B. who, disregarding beauty and amenities that were the inheritance of Dublin children, have filled in a large area of the strand and are polluting the rest. The sea is not so unsoilable as Oliver Gogarty suggested, for all its immensity.

At Sandycove there is another Martello Tower, made famous by James Joyce and now a museum housing letters and manuscripts which are well worth a visit. He lived here for a while in 1904, with his friend Oliver St. John Gogarty, whom he describes in the opening sentences of *Ulysses* as Buck

Mulligan (Joyce himself is 'Kinch'). The setting for Mulligan's early morning salutation to the world is the top of the tower with its gun emplacement in the centre.

'Stately, plump Buck Mulligan came from the stairhead, bearing a bowl of lather on which a mirror and a razor lay crossed. A yellow dressing-gown, ungirdled, was sustained gently behind him by the mild morning air. He held the bowl aloft and intoned:—Introibo ad altare Dei. Halted, he peered down the dark winding stairs and called coarsely—Come up, Kinch—Come up, you fearful Jesuit.

Solemnly he came forward and mounted the gun rest. He faced about and blessed gravely thrice the tower, the surrounding country and the awaking mountains.'

Beside the tower was the 'Forty Foot', a swimming place reserved exclusively for men which bore the ambiguously worded notice:

The rent of the tower was paid to the British Government in the person of the Secretary of State for War, who had it (and others equally useless) as a legacy from Mr. Pitt. They were built at the beginning of the nineteenth century as defences in case of an attempted invasion of Ireland by the French.

In 1904 Joyce was still torn between music and literature and had plans to tour England as a singer of Elizabethan songs. He failed to raise the necessary cash. A little earlier that same year he had been placed second to John McCormack, a very close second, according to the usual account, which says both were recalled but Joyce on principle refused the test of singing at sight.

Which brings me back to the 'cellist who once played in the pit orchestra of the Corinthian cinema. We met and became friends many years after the cinema orchestras had been put out of business by the introduction of sound films, and one night, when we were sitting together in his house sharing half a dozen Guinness, he started to talk of old times when he himself was a young man in the music profession. Joyce used to visit the house with other young artistes of the time, but he was not regarded as a gentleman because when offered a drink he asked for whiskey.

'It was very bad form and upset my mother', the 'cellist explained. 'Whiskey was only for older men. Joyce should have asked for sherry'.

That was Dublin at the turn of the century, a place where gentility had the men frozen from the neck up and the women (with admirable exceptions) from the waist down. Joyce and a few others did their best to liven it up. That same night the 'cellist showed me the programme of a concert he had played in in 1904 at the Antient Concert Rooms, in which the list of artistes included: *Mr. James A. Joyce* and *Mr. J. F. McCormack*.

On that occasion Joyce had boasted he would use the word 'arse' in public. He made good his boast when his turn came to mount the stage to sing one of Moore's melodies with the couplet:

> She is far from the land where her young hero sleeps
> And lovers are round her, sighing.

When Joyce came to this he fixed a grave eye on the 'cellist and in the second line made a simple alteration:

> She is far from the land where her young hero sleeps
> And lovers around *her arse sighing*.

James Joyce. '*Come up, Kinch—come up, you fearful Jesuit.*'

The audience hardly noticed, but for Joyce it eased the stifling pressures of a society that strove to trap his soul in its nets. Something of that seedy gentility still hung about the house in which I heard the story forty years later. It lingered in faded cushions, on beaded covers, in potted plants, in windows that were seldom opened and in heavily framed photographs of stiff-jointed, ceremonious relatives that stood on the piano top or hung from the walls. The women were excessively pious, much given to novenas and retreats; the men, in a decorous, unobtrusive and entirely gentlemanly fashion, often drank themselves to death.

2

> Grey brick upon brick
> Declamatory bronze
> On sombre pedestals
> O'Connell, Grattan, Moore
> And the brewery tugs and the swans
> On the balustraded stream
> And the bare bones of a fanlight
> Over a hungry door

That was how Louis MacNeice described the city the new State had inherited. Behind the hungry doors with their broken fanlights lay the world of poverty, roguery, yet undefeatable bravery that Sean O'Casey had begun to write about, before he left it because Yeats made the unforgivable blunder of rejecting his play *The Silver Tassie*. He never came back. I remember trying to persuade him in 1964 just before he died to be interviewed on television for the Yeats Centenary in 1965 and getting others who had influence with him to do likewise, but he was over eighty then and not interested. He was talking, he said, only to God.

'O'Casey is too old. His only conversations nowadays are with God (a pause) not solemn conversations, by the way—no, no . . . *Hilarious* conversations'.

Flat 3, 40 Trumlands Road, St. Marychurch, Torquay, Devon.
Tel. : Torquay 87766.

20 July . 1964

Jim Plunkett, Esq.

Dear Jim

I love to sign off from your proposal to join in the Television Remembrance to W. B. Yeats, much as I'd like to be one of the tributors. I am too old, almost blind now to do anything of this kind. It is "beyond the beyonds" for me now.

If you like, of course, you could use anything I've said of the great man in my biographical comments bout the poet. This is the most that I can do. My warm regards to good wishes to your family and you.

Sean

A letter from Sean O'Casey to the author.

And the swans had been given to the Liffey by Oliver St. John Gogarty, then a Senator of State, as a thanksgiving offering to the river God who had borne him safely to the other bank when he plunged into the freezing water to escape gunmen who were about to execute him in a house in Chapelizod. The swans on the river to-day are said to be the descendants of Gogarty's gift. As for the brewery tugs, they had funnels which could be folded back over the deck to allow sufficient clearance for passage under the bridges at high water and they carried cargoes of Guinness's stout for the daily consolation of decent citizens.

It was a noble city, if a bit decayed here and there. James Gandon's Custom House and his Four Courts still graced the riverside, despite civil war attempts to bomb the one and burn the other; her Georgian streets and squares gave her the air of an eighteenth century city. To-day age and the avarice of building speculators have torn great holes in the inheritance of elegance which Grattan's Parliament gave to the nation.

When I was six years of age or so we moved to a small flat in Upper Pembroke Street and I grew up in the shadow of those tall houses. Nearby was St. Stephen's Green where bands played to while away the warm afternoons of summer Sundays and old ladies fed the ducks on the pond from paper bags. On the south side of it stood the church of Cardinal Newman, who came to Dublin to found a Catholic University in 1854. Beside it in Number 86, Joyce had had his debate on the nature of beauty with the Dean of Studies, who was trying to light the fire.

'—"This fire before us", said the dean, "will be pleasing to the eye. Will it therefore be beautiful?"

—"In so far as it is apprehended by the sight, which I suppose means here aesthetic intellection, it will be beautiful. But Aquinas also says *Bonum est in quod tendit appetitus*. In so far as it satisfies the animal craving for warmth fire is a good. In hell, however, it is an evil."

—"Quite so", said the dean, "you have certainly hit the nail on the head."

He rose nimbly and went towards the door, set it ajar and said

Molly Malone

—"A draught is said to be a help in these matters".'

No. 86 had once been the house of Buck Whaley, celebrated in the 18th century for eccentricity. He made a journey to Jerusalem to play handball against its sacred walls and injured himself seriously when he jumped from the second floor over a passing carriage to win a wager. In his old age he reformed and devoted his time to writing his memoirs. Further up the street stood Iveagh House. Large crowds used to gather outside it every Holy Thursday to watch for the miraculous appearance of a cross on one of the windows. The story was that a Catholic servant girl had been caught telling her beads and had been thrown through the window to her death by her Protestant employer. I've seen that cross myself. It took the form of a blue glow which showed faintly on the glass and stretched the length and breadth of the window, which probably only proves you will see anything you have a mind to see provided you stare long and hard enough.

East of the Green stretched the long and gracious streets Joyce was to remember all his life: the haunt of W. B. Yeats, George Moore, Oliver St. John Gogarty, that brilliant company of writers and wits who walked and talked their uninterruptable way through the streets of my childhood—all, may I say, quite unknown to me. While they laboured daily at intellectual repartee and bombarded each other with limericks which (as someone said) were the only things that made conventional Dublin life bearable, I was of an age when I was still peddling a motor car round its squares and footpaths or sitting on the steps under the tall houses of Lower Leeson Street and wishing my father would come home from work. There was an ex-soldier who never passed me by. He was a burly, straight-backed man with a walking cane and a waxed moustache, who wasn't quite on his rocker. The routine was always the same. He'd do a left turn—slope arms in front of me and then with all the impact of a military band, he'd salute and declaim:

Two cigars
For two hussars
A pint and a bottle of stout

45

I would nod. This was as usual.
  Another salute:

> *Two sardines*
> *For two marines*
> *A pint and a bottle of stout*

Another nod. Another salute.

> *Two bugger-alls*
> *For two Donegals*
> *A pint and a bottle of stout*

'Bugger-all' meant 'nothing at all'. It was an expression, I knew, permissible only to the adult male.

There were a lot of ex-soldiers slightly off their heads in those days. One of them had a habit of directing the traffic; another used to let a yell out of him suddenly and start flinging imaginary hand grenades at imaginary machine gun nests.

At Leeson Street bridge, just up the road, we watched the barges on the Grand Canal which were still, in many cases, drawn by horses. The keeper opened the lock gates, the barge entered. Then the gates were closed and the waters rose until the barge was level with the bank again. The spume blew against our faces, the air smelled of decaying vegetation. The Grand Canal is another legacy of the eighteenth century, when it was built to provide easy transport to the midlands and the south-east. It connects Dublin with the rivers Shannon and Barrow, and carried passengers as well as cargo. The canal route opens up countryside which is sequestered and quiet, cut through by narrow roads of great charm, which are well worth the trouble of finding on the Ordnance map. The hotels which served the travellers are still to be seen, deserted now, in little canal villages which were once the focal point of bustle and excitement. The fare for travellers was cheap (twopence a mile as against threepence by road) and the accommodation, by eighteenth century standards of travel, commodious, but the pace only averaged two miles an hour. Robertstown in County Kildare, less than 20 miles from Dublin, is a canal village which

Sean O'Faolain . . . *who lashed at the obscurantism and false piety from his editorial chair on the magazine* The Bell.

still retains the atmosphere of the period. Each year, when they hold their Canal Fiesta, the river front is thronged with boats, and in the evening the hotel windows welcome travellers with a blaze of candlelight. Some time ago people who can put up with anything provided it isn't beautiful, came up with a scheme to drain the canal and lay a sewer along the bottom before filling it in for a roadway. It took a public campaign to save the Grand Canal. To-day it is being developed as a boating amenity.

The stretch of water from Leeson Street to Baggot Street Bridge has the quality of canal peace about it, a greenness, an ineffable pensiveness. Old trees line either side. Dogs nose along the grassy banks or bob out suddenly with sticks between their teeth; children on the narrow planks of the lock gates offer their bright young lives hourly to the raging whirlpools below; old men, by repetition reassured, I suppose, smoke their pipes and look on placidly; goats used to graze here too—whoever owned them. And yet it was always quiet and timeless, as though the children and the dogs, the old men and the goats and the crashing waters existed only on canvas. I associate it with Frank O'Connor the writer, who, I think, fell in love with it too. He was born in Cork but came to Dublin as a young man and he had memories of it from the time he lived on Pembroke Road, existing on a diet of coffee and buns which he got in Bewley's restaurant, because he was as yet too shy to venture into places more formal and sophisticated. When he died he was living in a flat at the Baggot Street end, where his study window provided him with a frame which allowed him, as it were, to hang the canal masterpiece on the wall. I had travelled monastic Ireland with him the previous summer and that was where I last spoke with him. I left him seated at his desk, the view in front of him, a script before him, his thoughts already bending inwards, the sunlight falling on the abstracted face with its high forehead and silver hair. He had the air of someone who had found where he belonged, not an easy thing for a writer to achieve in the Ireland of his time.

Both O'Connor and his friend and fellow writer Sean O'Faolain had been dedicated enemies of the obscurantism and false piety of the new order; O'Faolain especially, who lashed

THE BELL

EDITED BY PEADAR O'DONNELL

ASSOCIATE EDITOR, ANTHONY CRONIN.   BOOK SECTION, HUBERT BUTLER
MUSIC, JOHN BECKETT.

VOL. XVII.   NO. 3.   JUNE, 1951

CONTENTS

THE BELL is published monthly at 14 Lower O'Connell Street
Dublin.   Telephone 40951.   MSS. should be accompanied by a
stamped addressed envelope.   The yearly subscription is 19/6,
post free.

The Bell . . . *Bishop Browne of Galway publicly deplored what he called
'the venom of the* Irish Times *and the rancour of* The Bell'.

at its manifestations from his editorial chair on the magazine *The Bell*. Emigration, censorship, the pressure of Church influence on political legislation were exposed to a clearheaded and impartial criticism which was unthinkable from other sources. One such controversy was The Mother and Child Scheme, which had to do with the education of expectant mothers. The Government Department of Health had already announced the intention to introduce the Bill in a series of newspaper advertisements, but the Catholic Hierarchy, for reasons which seemed to be connected obscurely with their view of the sacredness of sex and birth, condemned it and the Government dropped the whole thing at the last moment. A proposal for Free Health services caused another uproar. The Hierarchy's view was that if the State paid for the treatment of a man's family in sickness, it deprived him of his right to do so himself and this, in some extraordinary interpretation of the moral law and the rights of the family, was an injustice to him. On the other hand, it was morally permissible for the parent to insure his family against sickness, provided he did so personally, from which it appeared that God's law countenanced insurance against ill-health provided it was handled by private enterprise or a voluntary society and not by the State. I remember one priest, otherwise a sane and reasonable man, who argued publicly that the Welfare State idea was immoral because it limited the field in which the Rich could exercise the virtue of charity in respect of the poor; in other words, a proportion of the population must be kept in the way of hardship so that the road to heaven might be made easier for those who were, materially, better endowed. This is a simple example of the tangle Catholic social thinking had got itself into, mainly through its terror of Socialist ideas. *The Bell* was in the lead in sorting out such thinking, despite the fulminations of people like Bishop Browne of Galway, who publicly deplored what he called 'the venom of the *Irish Times* and the rancour of *The Bell*'.

I'll let Patrick Kavanagh, the poet, have the last say on that stretch of canal, though as a Monaghan man, he has no right to it. But he lived on Pembroke Road and fell in love with it in his turn:

'I have been thinking of making my grave on the banks of the Grand Canal near Baggot Street Bridge where in recent days I re-discovered my roots. My hegira was to the Grand Canal bank where again I saw the beauty of water and green grass and the magic of light. It was the same emotion as I had known when I stood on a sharp slope in Monaghan . . . looking across to Slieve Gullion and South Armagh . . .

'This sonnet was inspired by two seats on the bank of the canal here "Erected to the memory of Mrs. Dermot O'Brien"' :

Commemorate me where there is water
Canal water preferably, so stilly
Greeny at the heart of summer. Brother
Commemorate me thus beautifully
Where by a lock niagarously roars
The falls for those who sit in the tremendous silence
Of mid-July. No one will speak in prose
Who finds his way to these Parnassian islands.
A swan goes by, head low with many apologies,
The bending light peeps through the eyes of bridges
And here! a barge comes bringing from Athy
And other far-flung towns mythologies.
O, memorial me with no hero-courageous
Tomb but just a canal bank seat for the passer-by

Since then his request has been fulfilled. A stone seat, erected by friends, stands on the south bank near the bridge, inscribed to his memory.

3

Dublin of the 18th century and later runs, roughly speaking, on a line north and south of O'Connell Bridge. The older city lies to the west, looking up Dame Street from the entrance to Trinity College. It had its origins in a settlement about a ford on the river from which it got one of its names, Baile Atha Cliath— the town of the hurdle ford. The name of 'Dublin' originates from its harbour, Dubh Linn—the Black Pool. The Danes were

the first to invade it. They sailed up the Liffey in their long boats at the beginning of the Ninth Century, used it for a while as a base for their raids into the countryside, then settled permanently in the city itself, which was ideally placed to be the hub of their scattered empire. Later in history the Normans came and the dispossessed Danish settlement moved across to the north bank of the river. With time the Normans adopted native ways, becoming (as a contemporary historian complained) 'more Irish than the Irish themselves'. In the thirteenth century Dublin Castle was built, first as a fortress for protection against the Irish clans of O'Byrne and O'Toole and then, as the invaders slowly consolidated themselves under the successive reigns of Henry VIII, Mary, Elizabeth, James I, as the principal seat of English Government in Ireland, its gates 'garnished with the grinning skulls of Irish Chiefs'. It continued so (though without the skulls) down to 1920.

From a huddle of houses in an area about Christ Church Cathedral, the city grew and accumulated its associations, its traditions, its mature personality, until fashion, after a period of almost a thousand years, began to draw the wealthy and influential away from it in the middle of the eighteenth century.

There is a difference in atmosphere between the two. The grace and elegance of the Georgian city, like much of the music of the same period, lift the soul into a realm of ordered beauty; a world where it is possible to be a poet without suffering pain, to labour without soiling the hands, to enlarge the spirit while the night watchmen ensure that the doors are safely guarded and all is well: indeed, that all continues for the best in the best of all possible worlds. In the older city this was never the case. Thirty years ago its ramshackle streets told you so. If they ever had grace and beauty, age had robbed them of it. Their houses, tottering above you like an old man on a stick, wore the wrinkled face of history—bitter history. The old city

Inishmurray (opposite above): *Today the remnants of the monastic movement lie scattered all over Ireland.*

Cashel (opposite below): *Tradition claims it was the dwelling place of the immortals . . .*

had known, for the most part, only the worst of all possible worlds. It had learned, nevertheless, to make the best of it. It recognised that life stains even the soul with sweat, as surely as revenge, betrayal, mishap, tyranny and murder will stain the streets with blood. And although it was already falling to bits when I first knew it, it was impossible to walk up High Street or Thomas Street, or to explore their tributaries to the right and to the left, without being conscious at once of defiant vitality and clamorous ghosts.

In the main thoroughfare all was bustle and business; the great drays of Power's Distillery and Guinness's Brewery clattered on the cobbles or filled the street with loud trundling and banging as they unloaded their wooden barrels into open gratings; the drivers of the number 21 trams banged hell out of the footbell at urchins who swore manfully back at them; in the shops the women haggled and bargained over what little they could spend; assistants with pencils behind their ears screwed bills and money together into little canisters mounted on overhead wires which whirred across the shops when they pulled the lever, and delivered their contents to the cashiers, where they were checked, the bills receipted and the change inserted and, when a trigger was pulled, were duly returned again. These wires where the little canisters crossed and re-crossed formed a miniature tramway system overhead. Outside the dogs nosed for discarded morsels under baskets of fish and vegetables and fruit. Across the road John's Lane Church with its spire high above the crowded pavements kept one watchful eye on heaven and the other on what was going on around it. Its interior, hushed and saturated with devotion, spoke of God in the accent of the poor. The flickering candles begged a thousand favours, the votive lamps, in glass cups of red and blue, bloomed their thanksgivings about the shrines of St. Rita and the Mother of Good Counsel. That Church was always busy with the prayers of women with shopping bags, or old men aware of the slow trickle of the sand.

Down the hill of Winetavern Street the secondhand clothes stalls served a society which, as someone had said, would have gone naked only everybody consented to be clad in someone else's cast-offs. There were wooden awnings over these shops to keep the sun from articles that had already faded beyond any possibility of further deterioration.

When you walked the back streets the houses were bent under the weight of families. They smelled of woodrot, over-crowding and grinding poverty. Some of them were very old indeed, with high gables and small-paned windows. The poles from their window sills fluttered gaily with drying clothes on wash days, while the afternoon hours added their own odours: the pungent aroma of the malting houses or, if the wind shifted to the wrong quarter, the heavy smell of O'Keeffe's the Knackers.

None of this bothered the children very much. They played their games in the afternoon streets and sang the songs that had come down to them through generations of childhood:

> The wind, the wind, the wind blows high
> The rain comes scattering from the sky
> Mary Kelly says she'll die
> If she doesn't get the fella with the marble eye
>
> He is handsome, he is pretty
> He is the fairest in this city
> He is courting one, two, three
> O, please tell me, who is he?

But when the streets grew hushed and the evening wind brought the river odour to mingle with the smells of decay and poverty, the brooding houses seemed stricken not only by time but by old remembrances. Everywhere had its ghosts and its associations; the squares of the weavers who once toiled long hours under the eyes of their masters, or sallied down to the bridges on a public holiday for a faction fight with the butchers of the north bank. Thomas Street, where Lord Edward Fitzgerald was captured and who later escaped execution only by dying of the wounds inflicted on him in the struggle; the open space at Cornmarket where Newgate Prison once stood. It was a place of dismal history, some of its cells half under water, its prisoners dependent on the charity of the passerby, and the gallows the usual end to their misery. Here the eve of an execution was made the occasion for a wild party by the friends of the doomed man, provided they could raise the money for a carouse. After the execution the friends and the sack-'em-up men (body snatchers) would fight for the corpse, and they commemorated their comrades in slang ballads of their underworld:

The night before Larry was stretched
The boys they all paid him a visit
A bait in their sacks too they fetched
They sweated their dud till they riz it.
For Larry was ever the lad
When a boy was condemned to the squeezer
Would fence all the duds that he had
To help a poor friend in a sneezer
And warm his gob 'fore he died

I'm sorry, dear Larry, says I
To see you in this situation
And blister my limbs if I lie
I'd as lief it had been my own station
'Ochone, it's all over', says he
'For the neckcloth I'll be forced to put on
And by this time tomorrow you'll see
Poor Larry as dead as a mutton'
Because, why, his courage was good

So moving these last words he spoke
We all vented our tears in a shower
For my part, I thought my heart broke
To see him cut down in his flower
On his travels we watched him next day
Oh, the throttler, I thought I could kill him:
But Larry not one word did say
Nor changed till he came to 'King William'
Then, musha—his colour turned white

When he came to the nubbling chit
He was tucked up so neat and so pretty
The rumbler jogged off from his feet
And he died with his face to the city
He kicked too, but that was all pride
For soon you might see 'twas all over:
Soon after the noose was untied
And at darky we waked him in clover
And sent him to take a ground sweat.

You could go down the winding steps past the old Norman church in High Street and they led you to St. Audoen's Gate which was already there when Edward Bruce encamped outside the city. It is the only surviving gate. Below Christ Church Cathedral, clearances have restored what time had long hidden away and the old Danish city is being uncovered after a thousand years; their causeways, their huts and shops, the artefacts of their daily living: combs and needles, household utensils, bracelets and ornamental pins, the drawing of a Viking ship, a child's piggy bank with its coins, all the bits and pieces the earth guards for posterity when the captains and the warriors have set sail for eternity on the last raid of all.

Bridge Street, nearby, joins the quayside at a point which, two thousand years ago, may have been the centre of the original settlement about the ford, Baile Atha Cliath itself. In more recent history Mullett's Pub stood here. The knives for the Phoenix Park murderers are said to have been given out in its back snug during Parnell's time. Mullett himself got into trouble by hoisting the green flag with the gold harp above his premises when the rest of the city was smothered in Union Jacks in honour of Queen Victoria's visit. Mullett's has gone, but the Brazen Head, the oldest tavern in Dublin, where the men of 1798 plotted and Robert Emmet was a frequent visitor, is still in business. In the thirties, on the pretence of wanting to dine, it was sometimes possible to get in to drink after official licensing hours, provided you could allay the justifiable

The Brazen Head. *It whispers of conspiracies.*

suspicions of the old lady who guarded the door. If she suspected her visitors she kept the door bolted while she shouted out a pointed inquiry:

'Are yiz students or gentlemen?'

The last time I was there the wall of the gents toilet acknowledged history in an unusual way. One highly educated piece of graffiti declared:

Molly Malone

Joannus Canavanus
hic erat 1966

Another, underneath, was equally specific:

Robert Emmet was here too—1803

The Brazen Head has retained the aura of its past in a distinctive way. It whispers of conspiracies.

Further up, in Thomas Street, St. Catherine's Church glooms above the traffic in what was once a market place. Blackened with age, it too remembers blood, and the head of Robert Emmet held high above its spiked railings for the mob to gape at.

It is true of the Irish that, while they respect victory, they have a warmer admiration for failure, possibly because they understand it better. Certainly Emmet's name lived and was loved in the city I grew up in. His rebellion was a pathetic little affair, so amateurish that it was crushed almost before it started. But he died for it, which was noble; and he achieved a magnificent speech, which in popular regard, was even more admirable. It hung, as I said earlier, in many a humble household, with an engraving of himself above it, addressing the hated Lord Norbury, 'the Hanging Judge'.

'. . . I do not fear to approach the Omnipotent Judge to answer for the conduct of my whole life; am I then to be appalled and falsified by a mere remnant of mortality here— by you, too, although if it were possible to collect all the innocent blood that you have shed in your unhallowed ministry in one great reservoir, your lordship might swim in it . . . '

Emmet, expelled from Trinity College for his championship of the hated and alarming sentiments of liberty, equality and fraternity, decided on rebellion as the only hope of justice. He and kindred souls pamphleteered and armed secretly. His main arsenal was in Marshalsea Lane, across the road from St. Catherine's. An accidental explosion gave the secret away and forced him to premature action, so that his supporters could

not be rallied in sufficient numbers and when he took to the streets it was at the head of an untrained mob, which was engaged and quickly scattered. He might still have saved his life if he had taken adequate precaution; instead he delayed to take his farewell of his sweetheart, Sarah Curran. He was captured, made his long and magnificent speech and was hanged and beheaded, a noble young gentleman who was to become the idol of his city and to live in popular balladry as the darlin' of Erin:

> Bold Robert Emmet, the darling of Erin
> Bold Robert Emmet will die with a smile
> Farewell companions both loyal and daring
> I lay down my life for the Emerald Isle

Another chapter of the Emmet tragedy was written in No. 2 Little Elbow Lane, off the Coombe, where Anne Devlin, his servant, died in a squalid tenement room in 1851. At the age of twenty-two she had suffered imprisonment, torture and half hanging rather than inform on him. Her brother was done to death at her side, her parents were cast into prison. When it was all over she was released and soon forgotten by all but a handful of people who could do little for her. One of them was Luke Cullen, a seaman who took to the religious life and became a Carmelite Brother. He sought her out, relieved her want whenever he could out of his own meagre resources and encouraged her to dictate her prison experiences to him.

'Early the following morning after the execution I was ordered (from Kilmainham Gaol) into a coach which drove off rapidly to the Birmingham Tower at the Castle. The jailer sat in front of me with a pair of pistols partly concealed. A soldier sat each side of me with a drawn bayonet. Coming down to St. Catherine's Church in Thomas Street, the coach stopped at a signal from the jailer. The windows were on a sudden let down. I looked out.

Robert Emmet (opposite). *It is true of the Irish that, while they respect victory, they have a warmer admiration for failure.*

'Horror came over me when I perceived the blood of Mr. Emmet on the scaffold where his head had been cut off. Dogs and pigs were lapping his blood from between the paving stones.'

The coach passed on, the city put away its hopes in their well worn hiding place, Anne Devlin found a hovel in its back streets to abide in and hunger in for almost fifty more years.

And W. B. Yeats, when his own hour of disillusionment and despair of his contemporaries caused him to write the epitaph of his hopes, found his thoughts drawn back to that nobility and self-sacrifice.

> Was it for this the wild geese spread
> The grey wing upon every tide
> For this that all that blood was shed
> For this Edward Fitzgerald died
> And Robert Emmet and Wolfe Tone
> All that delirium of the brave?
> Romantic Ireland's dead and gone
> It's with O'Leary in the grave.

Yeats wrote too soon. There was another act to go.

While Anne Devlin supported existence in Elbow Lane by taking in washing from respectable families, a young poet, James Clarence Mangan, who had been born in the year of Emmet's Rebellion (1803) was living in the shell of a house in Chancery Lane. The place of door and windows was supplied by a huge gap in the broken wall, through which 'the winds and rains blew in on all sides, and whistled and howled through the winter nights like the voices of unquiet spirits'. He was the son of a grocer who had ruined himself and his family through generosity and drink, traditional outlets of a city where rich and poor alike were usually either roistering (often enough in each other's company) or plotting to murder one another. For schooling, while there was still money to pay for it, he attended Mr. Courtney's Academy in Darby Square; when the collapse of his father's business came he got work as apprentice to a scrivener. Of the poets of the Nation newspaper, to which he contributed, he was unquestionably the best. Much of what he wrote found its way into the classrooms of childhood about which I spoke earlier. His vision of Ireland was suitably romantic, as was his preoccupation with that code of honour and virtue which he believed was to be found in the golden age of history. That he did so as a consolation for the brutality and viciousness of the world he had to live in was glossed over, as were the poems which confessed his own dissipations and guilt.

> '. . . I hear all night as through a storm
> Hoarse voices calling, calling
> My name upon the wind—
> All omens monstrous and appalling
> Affright my guilty mind
>
> I exult alone in one wild hour—
> That hour in which the red cup drowns
> The memories it anon renews
> In ghostlier guise, in fiercer power—
> Then Fancy brings me golden crowns
> And visions of all brilliant hues
> Lap my lost soul in gladness
> Until I wake again
> And the dark lava-fires of madness
> Once more sweep through my brain

Mangan's life, in spite of his craving for virtue and nobility (or perhaps, indeed, because of it), his prayers, his repentance, his remorse, was a progress through drink and drug addiction to death of cholera at the age of forty-six. He was never able to escape the sickness of soul which had its beginnings in the brutal insecurities of his childhood:

'In my boyhood I was haunted by an indescribable feeling of something terrible. It was as though I stood in the vicinity of some tremendous danger, to which my apprehensions could give neither form nor outline. What it was I knew not: but it seemed to include many kinds of pain and bitterness— baffled hopes—and memories full of remorse . . . Like Bonnet, whose life was embittered by the strange notion that he saw *an honest man* continually robbing his house, I suffered as much from my inability to harmonize my thoughts and feelings as from the very evil itself that I dreaded. Such was my condition from my sixth to my sixteenth year'.

In later life Mangan worked long hours in a solicitor's office where by evening time the perpetually smoking chimney had so impregnated the atmosphere with its sulphurous fog that he would almost choke to death. In the same fragment of autobiography, written while he was lodging in Fishamble Street, he deplores 'the coarse ribaldry, the vile and vulgar oaths and the brutal indifference' of his office companions. That these were weapons against the pressures of environment developed in self-defence by men who have no other resources never occurred to Mangan, for the reason that in his case Nature's usual foresight had failed to provide them. Without them his life was blighted. To a stranger who, meeting him in a country lane, praised the scenery and the setting sun, Mangan answered:

'I have pleasure in nothing and I admire nothing. I hate scenery and suns. I see nothing in nature but what is fallen and ruined'.

It might have been an answer from the great Jonathan Swift himself, who had been Dean of St. Patrick's Cathedral over a hundred years before Mangan's birth. They shared the same city, the same vision of the world and the same loathing of its corruptions: the essential difference being that while Mangan sought to find shelter, the Dean quickly learned how to lob back the hand grenades. In Mangan's case literature gained modestly; in Swift's, magnificently. Yet for many young poets of my youth Mangan was the more beloved of the two, a lost creature stumbling to defeat through 18th century streets, in a ragged cloak and a broken-crowned hat, with a voluminous and useless umbrella under his arm. His bust in Stephen's Green was much reverenced and at least two of my contemporaries wrote plays about him.

If Mangan sparked the imagination of the younger poets, Swift lived permanently in the affections of the ordinary people

—I mean, of course, the people of the older city. They spoke of him as though they remembered him, which is the way of living legend. In his lifetime his influence was enormous. There is a story that a noisy mob that gathered near the Cathedral to await an eclipse of the moon dispersed without question when a message was sent to them that it had been postponed on the Dean's instructions.

He was born in 1667 in Hoey's Court, which stood behind the Castle walls and within a stone's throw of the Cathedral he was to spend much of his life in. The house has gone, but a turn through the archway off Castle Street and down the steps brings one to where it once stood. At the age of six he was sent to St. John's College in Kilkenny and eight years later he entered Trinity College, where after an undistinguished career, he got his Bachelor of Arts degree *Speciali Gratia*—more or less for God's sake. In 1689 he became secretary to Sir William Temple of Moor Park in Surrey. Here he met Esther Johnson. She was only eight years old, but she was to become the Stella in the Stella-Vanessa enigma which Swift scholars have not yet satisfactorily untangled. Swift was ordained in 1694, obtaining first the living of Kilroot in Co. Antrim and then the benefice of Laracor in Co. Meath. While he was there Sir William died, leaving £1,500 to Stella. Swift suggested she should come and live in Ireland and she did so (with the exception of one short visit to England) for the rest of her life.

During the years from 1701–1714 he spent much time in England, becoming a leading propagandist for the Tory Party. For his services he was offered the Deanery of St. Patrick's Cathedral. He had expected more and was bitterly disappointed. Again he was followed to Dublin, this time by a girl with whom he had become acquainted in his London years, Esther Van Homrigh. She took up residence in Celbridge, Co. Kildare, in a house she had inherited. Esther became the Vanessa of Swift's life and the triangle—if it was a triangle—was complete.

Swift, although he was born in Dublin, hardly regarded himself as Irish, believing with Wellington (whose birthplace was Dublin also) that being born in a stable didn't make you a horse. Yet he became sharply critical of English policy towards

Georgian doorways, Dublin. *I grew up in the shadow of those tall houses.*

Ireland and identified himself closely with Ireland's welfare. In 1720, in answer to English embargoes and restrictions on Irish made goods, he published his 'Proposal for the Universal Use of Irish Manufacture' in which his typical advice was that Ireland should burn everything English—except her coal. When the King's mistress, the Duchess of Kendal, got a patent to supply Ireland with coinage and sold the concession to an ironmaster of Birmingham called William Wood, Swift issued his Drapier's letters, which painted such an exaggerated picture of the effects on merchant and poor man alike if the debased coinage were accepted that it had to be withdrawn from circulation. The Government knew who 'M. B. Drapier' really was but Swift's popularity was such that they were afraid to lay a finger on him. In 1729, moved to cold anger by the sufferings of the poor, he issued his *A Modest Proposal: for preventing the*

Children of Poor People from being a Burthen to their Parents, or the Country, and for making them Beneficial to the Publick.

The proposal was that the poor should be encouraged to breed some of their children as food for the nation, a system which would supply meat for the rich and be a source of income for the parents . . . 'I grant this food will be somewhat dear, and therefore very *proper for landlords* who, as they have already devoured most of the Parents, seem to have the best title for the children. Infants' flesh will be in Season throughout the Year, but more plentiful in *March,* and a little before and after, for we are told by a grave Author, an eminent *French* Physician, that *Fish being a prolifick Dyet,* there are more Children born in *Roman Catholick Countries* about nine months after Lent, than at any other Season: Therefore reckoning a Year after Lent, the Markets will be more glutted than usual, because the number of *Popish Infants,* is at least three to one in this Kingdom, and therefore it will have one other Collateral advantage by lessening the number of *Papists* among us'.

The fact that Swift wrote his pamphlet in the style of the public reformers of the time (and there were many proposals for public reform) using their language and their reasoning methods, misled a number of people, who missed the savage irony and were deeply shocked.

The Cathedral itself dates from the early thirteenth century, although the site it occupies was an ecclesiastical one long before the Norman invasion. Some years before Swift, Cromwell's troops stabled their horses in the aisles; shortly after his death a misguided bishop did it a more permanent disservice by perching an incongruous spire on its honest, 14th century tower. Swift's altruism was more practical. He left his life savings to found St. Patrick's Hospital for the mentally ill, denying at the same time, with his usual gruffness, that charity or compassion had anything at all to do with it.

> He left what little wealth he had
> To build a house for fools and mad
> And showed by one satiric touch
> No nation wanted it so much

There was a further satirical touch before he died in 1745. Swift, in his dotage, was still the wonder of the streets and the alleyways: his manservant found a way to supplement his wages by letting parties of the mob in at a charge of sixpence a head to gape their fill at the drooling and senile old man, whose rages and ramblings were famous throughout the land. In that way the dying Gulliver became a showpiece for the Yahoos he had relieved and befriended.

Both Swift and Stella lie at rest in the Cathedral.

Beyond the old city, on high ground above the north bank of the river Liffey, is Phoenix Park, 1,752 acres of open parkland. Since the 17th century it has been set aside as a deer park and pleasure ground. The Duke of Ormonde, who secured it for the citizens, had to fight the Duchess of Cleveland for it; she was demanding it from Charles II at the time in return, no doubt, for services rendered. When she found herself out-manoeuvred by Ormonde, she expressed the fervent hope that she might live to see him hanged. Ormonde, in reply, told her his deepest wish was to live long enough to see her old. Compliments fly (as they say) when the Quality meet.

The Duchess has long since admitted to age, and today the citizens have their choice of pleasures, which range from sitting on the benches in a well-earned trance to the complicated rituals of the Polo ground. Almost everything that can happen in the way of recreation happens in the park; girls play camogie, boys play Gaelic and Soccer football, cricket bats connect with a pock from time to time and evoke a thin crackle of applause; there are schools of equestrian ladies and gentlemen in full canonicals; there are tight-jawed inscrutable trainers exercising greyhounds. The children take elephant rides in the Zoo, the oars of the racing crews flash in swift unison on the Liffey. Beyond the activity of the parkland, beyond the trees and the silver ribbon of the Liffey and the crowding roofs of houses, the Dublin and Wicklow mountains curve upwards in coloured and shapely grace. They are another world. They guard a quite different tradition.

3

The King O'Toole

MY paternal grandmother, a little woman who surprised me now and then by her free and easy use of strong language, confessed to me once that she believed in fairies. I was a sceptical child and it came to me as a great shock. Ghosts were all right, practically everybody knew someone who knew someone else who had seen one. The Banshee I accepted (I believed I had heard her keening one night myself). But fairies were beyond the sensible limit. I asked her what in God's name led her into such a strange notion. She told me she had seen them.

'Where?' I asked.

'In Glencullen', she said, 'when I was a young girl and I in the fields milking the cows of a summer's morning. I'd see them riding down the mountain on their horses'.

'What horses?' I asked.

'White horses mostly', she said, 'though there was the odd brown one'.

'And what were they like?' I asked, determined not to let her away with it.

'Little men', she said, 'with green tunics and scarlet breeches. Do you not believe in fairies yourself?'

'I do not', I said.

'Ah, well', she said, taking the poker to stir the fire, a thing she always did when people downfaced her, 'maybe there's none any longer. There's many a wonder gone out of the world since I myself was a child'.

Nevertheless the next time I was in Glencullen I kept a sharp eye out, in case there might be a bit of excitement I might miss. I followed a little mountain stream for a long way up the hillside. The water was golden brown from bog and sunlight, it had whorls and rapids where thick clouts of foam spun round and round. The air smelled of gorse and thorn bushes, a warm, hungry smell. It looked like a good place for any band of fairies that knew their business, but there were none. The odd rabbit popped off with a flash of white scut, an old goat with a beard chased me through a clump of nettles, which raised blisters on my bare legs. When I escaped I rubbed them with dock leaves to stop the stinging. My grandmother, I decided, must have been a particularly gullible child. There was tea when I got back with boiled eggs, homemade bread and jam and farmhouse butter. That is the first memory of many that still remain with me of the Dublin-Wicklow mountains. In those days you travelled by horse and trap, a slow, swaying way of doing it, with the roadside trees and the stone walls meandering by and the crunching sound of the wheels in your ears.

They are very beautiful, those mountains, much more to me than mere landscape. The shorter journeys were through Whitechurch and Pine Forest to Glencullen, where there was always a stop at Fox's Pub, strong refreshment for the men, lemonade and biscuits for me; or by Dundrum and the Scalp to Enniskerry, with the same trimmings at journey's end. But the real adventure was to travel over Sallygap to Glendalough by the military road. It was built in an effort to root out the rebels after the rising of 1798 and goes like an arrow into the hills.

It leads past the Yellow House at Rathfarnham, where the soldiery stopped for refreshment when escorting Anne Devlin and her parents and relatives to prison, through Ballyboden and then to the right and left as it climbs for the summit of the Featherbed Mountain. The Hellfire Club can be visited en route by taking the roadway constructed through the new plantations by the Forestry Department. The entrance is at a point just

above an old house which is now the Hellfire Art Gallery and I
have noticed recently that it is becoming a favourite evening
walk with Dublin people in the mood for exercise. The road
climbs steadily towards the summit, revealing fine views of
Pine Forest and Tibradden mountain on the left and Dublin Bay
and coastline to the east. The building itself has a look of ancient
villainies about it. Hellfire Club was a wild rendezvous for the
bucks and blades of the aristocracy in the 18th century, a place
for drinking and gambling, and for the rape of abducted
heiresses, who felt they had to redeem their virtue by consenting
to marriage with the young rake responsible. The bucks found
it a quick way to restore an ill-spent inheritance. They used to
celebrate Black Masses here too, or so local gossip had it. Then
one day during a game of cards someone looked under the
table at the legs of the stranger who had joined the company
and found he had a cloven hoof. It was the Devil himself. This
appearance seems to have given the place a bad name. Anyway,
it was allowed to fall into ruins. The story tempted some friends
and myself to sleep in the ruins one Hallowe'en many years ago,
when we were all about fourteen or fifteen years of age. The
wind howled in the chimneys, the ruins creaked and groaned,
everything seemed propitious, but the Devil failed to turn up.
He had grown used to more aristocratic company.

At the summit of the Featherbed Mountain the gradient of
the military road levels out for some miles and the mountains
of Wicklow spread out before one. Glenasmole, the Glen of the
Thrushes, lies down the steep slope to the right. Legend has it
that Ossian, who had gone to the Land of the Ever Young with
his young wife Niamh, conceived a longing to talk to Fionn
and his companions and set off to find them, with a warning
from Niamh not to set foot on the soil but to remain all the time
in the saddle. In his search for Fionn he came to Glenasmole,
where he found a group of men struggling to move a great rock.
Ossian stooped from his horse to help them but his saddleband
broke and he toppled to the ground. Suddenly the years he had
spent in the Land of the Ever Young descended on him like an
avalanche and Ossian, the poet hero, became a feeble old man.

He found out then that his sojourn in the land of the Ever

The Military Road . . . *levels out and the mountains of Wicklow spread out before one.*

Young, which had seemed but a month or so, had been over a hundred years. Fionn and his hero companions were all dead, the Christian Faith had replaced their pagan beliefs and customs. St. Patrick met him and informed him that Fionn and the Fionna were all in Hell for their sins. Ossian replied that if that were so, Hell was the place he would wish to go to himself. All this gave rise to an argument between them which forms one of the livelier sections of the old story cycle. The truth is the Irish could never make up their minds which they liked better, the new Christianity or the old pagan heroes and their deeds. I remember a very old man from the west of Ireland who was upbraided by his parish priest for constantly standing at the door of the church on Sundays instead of going inside to hear mass.

'John', said the priest to him, 'will you go right into the church like a good man, and for God's sake and your soul's sake fix your thoughts for a little while on the world to come'.

'Easy on, Father, easy', said the old man, 'let's have wan world at a time'.

It is only fair to add that there are valleys in other parts of the country, including Sligo, that lay claim to the same Ossian incident.

Further on, the memorial to the left of the road marks the spot where the body of Noel Lemass was found, a victim of fratricidal hates. The cross, rising above the melancholy emptiness of brown bogland, is as evocative a symbol of Irish history as any ancient tower or cromlech, a reminder of the civil war years, of mountain ambushes, of a Government forced to live in Government Buildings for security, of Kevin O'Higgins taking exercise on the roof in the darkness after his day's work as Minister for Justice and afraid to strike a match to light a cigarette because it was certain to attract a sniper's bullet. Jimmy O'Dea, the Irish comedian, who had been an optician as a young man, once told me of identifying Noel Lemass's body by a pair of spectacle frames found beside it: he had supplied them only a few days before his disappearance.

The Barracks at Glencree is one of a number of strongholds built after the 1798 rising. One of its commanders was Sir John Moore, later commemorated in the well-known poem 'The Burial of Sir John Moore at Corunna'. He parleyed here with Michael Dwyer, the rebel leader, giving him safe conduct for the purpose. Later, under the Oblate Fathers, it became a Reformatory. After the second world war it was used for a time to house refugee children from Europe. In the cemetery across the road lie the bodies of German airforce men who crashed over Ireland, and sailors whose bodies were washed up on the Irish coast during two world wars, and who were brought together here for their final rest.

The Barracks has witnessed its fill of human loneliness and suffering. It commands a superb view of the surrounding country. Glencree Valley stretches seven miles or so to the south east, with War Hill and Maulin Mountain rising steeply to the south and Sugar Loaf mountain marking its farthest boundary. The glen itself is secluded and fertile in its lower reaches, with the Glencree river winding along its floor, fed by the narrow streams from the slopes, which become miniature waterfalls and fill the air with the sound of tumbling waters after heavy rain. Many centuries ago, when it was still covered with oak forests, it was a Royal Park for English Sovereigns, who eventually in the way of Sovereigns, stripped it of its trees for the building of their mansions. To-day much of it has been replanted with fir trees. At first they looked well as they marched in regular green ranks up the mountain slopes: now there are far too many of them, not only in Glencree but elsewhere. Their monotonous uniformity has robbed many individualistic landscapes of their distinctive character.

Lady Wilde used to spend summer vacations here with Willie and Oscar when they were young children, in a house called Crone which was then occupied by a family called Evans, and later, when I got to know it myself, by Harpurs. There was a rocking chair there in which she was said to have nursed young Oscar:

'Behold me, Speranza, rocking a cradle at this present writing in which lies my second son, a babe of one month old . . . He is to be called Oscar Fingal Wilde. Is not that grand, misty and Ossianic?'

Whatever about 'grand', Oscar was never shaped to be either misty or Ossianic. There is a story that Lady Wilde and the two children used to attend Mass in the Glencree Barracks (by then turned into a reformatory) and that she prevailed on a Father Fox who was stationed there to baptise them as Roman Catholics. Official quarters later denied 'any record or tradition in Glencree or district that Oscar Wilde was baptised a Catholic there'. Perhaps the answer is that when someone wishes the event to be kept secret, as Lady Wilde did, it is unlikely to be done in a manner which will allow it to become part of local tradition. If he did not baptise the children, what had Father Fox to gain by asserting he had?

The King O'Toole

2

Until his death in the Spring of 1944, Glencree was the home of Joseph Campbell, a poet who produced a number of works which are better known in Ireland than is the name of the man who wrote them. One of these *The Wicklow Hills* was as inevitable during a sentimental public house session at one time as was *Roll Out the Barrel* in a later generation. My father used to sing it at parties, I remember, while his cronies and butties joined in harmony with every appearance of broken and bleeding hearts. Yet the odd thing is that the melody was composed for the words (at Campbell's request) by a very scholarly lady, a Fellow of the Royal College of Organists and the politely bred daughter of a clergyman. I suppose neither anticipated it would take a high place in the public house repertoire. Despite all that, as songs of the kind go, I think it's a fine one.

Another of his verses, *My Lagan Love* is superb, as is the air it is fitted to. It is highly popular. So too, are his verses about the 18th century College Sizar's encounter with the Spanish Lady.

As I walked down through Dublin City
At the hour of twelve in the night
Who should I spy but a Spanish Lady
Washing her feet by candlelight?
First she dipped them, then she dried them
Over a fire of ambery coal.
Never in all my life did I see
A maid so neat about the sole.

I stopped to peep, but the Watchman passed
And says: young fellow, the night is late
Get home to bed or I'll wrastle you
At a double trot through the Bridewell Gate!
So I waved a kiss to the Spanish Lady
Hot as the fire of cramesy coal
I've seen dark maids, though never one
So white and neat about the sole.

O, she's too rich for a Poddle swaddy
With her tortoise comb and mantle fine,
A Hellfire buck would fit her better,
Drinking brandy and claret wine.
I'm just a decent College sizar,
Poor as a sod of smouldery coal;
And how would I dress the Spanish Lady
And she so neat about the sole?

O, she'd make a mott for the Provost Marshal
Or a wife for the Mayor on his coach so high,
Or a queen of Andalusia
Kicking her heel in the Cardinal's eye.
I'm blue as cockles, brown as herrings
Over a grid of glimmery coal
And all because of the Spanish Lady
So mortial neat about the sole.

I wandered north, and I wandered south
By Golden Lane and Patrick's Close,
The Coombe, Smithfield and Stoneybatter,
Back to Napper Tandy's house.
Old age has laid its hand upon me
Cold as a fire of ashy coal
And where is the lovely Spanish Lady
That maid so neat about the sole?

Joseph Campbell was very much a poet of Place, whose work enriches the landscape of County Wicklow, his chosen home. 'The ancient district of Cualann (he wrote) belonged, for the most part, to the County of Wicklow . . . wild and unspoilt, a county of cairn crowned hills and dark, watered valleys, it bears even to this day something of the freshness of the heroic dawn'. And as he walked it the old sagas and stories lived for him:

> The burning inn at the crossways
> The fian tracking the boar,

The queen riding northward
With her horseboys and women—
Are the thought in your heart
The earth under your feet.

Although he never found the distinction of style which sets
J. M. Synge—another writer who drew deeply on County
Wicklow for his material—in a place apart, Campbell had the
same obsession with the simple realities of life. 'Irishry' is a
poet's album of characters who travelled the country roads
fifty or sixty years ago, or who worked in the fields and the hills:
fiddlers, shepherds, ploughmen, a blind man at a Fair, a cobbler,
a rag-and-bone man. The Road Mender, the Bone-Setter, the
Horse-Breaker, inspired his verse and through it, although time
and change have eclipsed almost all of them, their ghostly figures
still people the countryside. He records an imbecile boy
employed to scare the crows, or a chimney sweep going by in
winter time.

His face, his brush, his body
As black as night
Against the snowy uplands
And dancing light.

Or the Osier-Sellers travelling through the mountain pass
at late evening.

In the long sun shadows
They went the mountain road:
A blind man and his son,
And two asses with their load

Fresh green river osiers
Sweeping the frosty ground
The four barths and straw tackle
Worth, maybe, a pound.

Not that gold would buy
The osiers or the straw:

For one grows by man's cunning
The other by God's law

Nor that order outweighs
The strange beauty they made
The two men and their beasts
Following an ancient trade

In the long moon shadows
They will come again
Sober like decent Irish
Or drunk with their gain

Campbell was deeply involved with Wicklow landscape and its associations, so that its saints and heroes, its people, its wild life and natural features move him to poems which, if minor, have the essential truth of poetry. His voice, within its range, is a unique one, fully committed to its chosen world and for that very reason both revealing and rewarding.

If Campbell found peace in the contemplation of his Wicklow valleys and mountains, and was content to live quietly in its solitudes where (as he tells us) curlew and stonechat, ewes and lambs, the shy deer, the stoats and rats

Harbingers of high thoughts and fathers of poems
Come to my haggard gate, my very doorstep

J. M. Synge, equally solitary as a man, moved restlessly through its glens and desolate places in search of two things: a new literary idiom and the answer to what he regarded as the unforgivable insult—Death.

Still South I went, and West and South again
Through Wicklow from the morning to the night,
And far from cities and the sights of men
Lived with the sunshine and the moon's delight

The King O'Toole

I knew the stars, the flowers and the birds
The grey and wintry sides of many glens
And did but half-remember human words
In converse with the mountains moors and fens.

The poem tends to gutter out in the last two lines, but it expresses, nevertheless, Synge's gait of going. In Wicklow, as in Kerry and on the Aran Islands, he grasped at what was offered in scenery, in solitude, in the instinctive life of bird and beast, in the customs of simple people and their way of speech, hoping to forge from these elements a truth to live by. Unlike Campbell he was Anglo-Irish by birth and background, with a forbidding number of clergymen and bishops among his ancestors on both sides. His home life was so smothered in strict religious observance that he had no option as an artist but to reject it. At first music seemed to offer escape. He studied to be a professional violinist and his first creative efforts were in the field of musical composition. These included violin pieces and several attempts at a string quartet, which may still be examined in manuscripts which have been preserved. Although as music these early attempts are remarkably unimpressive, Synge lavished sufficient industry on them to alarm his family and to be warned by one of his pompous brothers that professional musicians invariably took to drink.

He was living at 4 Orwell Park (Dublin) at the time. His brothers regarded him as some kind of freak; his mother, a woman of extreme evangelical views, tried to fix his thoughts on the danger of being damned for all eternity. For a while she succeeded. Then one day, while he was still a youth, he read some sentences by Darwin on the similarity between a bird's wing and a man's hand and the shock killed his careful biblical upbringing stone dead. After that, music claimed him so exclusively that he went to Germany to study it. But he lacked the nerve for public performance and drifted to Paris where W. B. Yeats found him studying French literature. Either because Yeats himself, egged on by Maud Gonne, was up to his artistic neck in nationalistic fervour at the time, or because of a

79

moment of true poetic prescience, Yeats urged him to seek his material in the life of his own country. Synge accepted the advice.

Eventually, like Wordsworth, he began to find Truth in the observation of nature and in the drama of daily events. Unlike him, he transformed the turns of everyday speech into a literary idiom of unique musical and rhythmic range. And did so, on his own admission, by studying the conversation of unlettered people:

> 'In writing *The Playboy of The Western World*, as in my other plays, I have used one or two words only that I have not heard among the country people of Ireland, or spoken in my own nursery before I could read the newspapers . . . When I was writing *The Shadow of the Glen* . . . I got more aid than any learning could have given me from the chink in the floor of the old Wicklow house where I was staying, that let me hear what was being said by the servant girls in the kitchen'.

I have reason to believe the 'old Wicklow house' he refers to was 'Uplands', to the left of the road from Roundwood to Annamoe, the little village where an earlier writer, Laurence Sterne, created a sensation as a child by falling through a mill-race while the mill was going and getting out unhurt.

Above Glencree, on the road to Sallygap, is the lonely cottage Synge frequently stayed in. When I first knew it the owner could still produce a visitors' book with his name inscribed in it. Behind it lower Lough Bray nestles below the dark cliffs of Kippure mountain, and in front of its door the valley of Glencree displays its variety; heathered slopes strewn with giant boulders, gorse bushes with their yellow flowers, rowan trees that in season hang their red berries above brown mountain torrents. The remnants of the old oak forest still spread in sparse patches here and there, the fertile fields make a patchwork in its lower reaches, the river itself wanders the valley floor between bramble and fern and bright beaches of river sand.

From here he heard the stone cutters at work on the hillside, or talked to the herds as their small Wicklow collies rounded in

J. M. Synge's Cottage. *Above Glencree, on the road to Sallygap, is the lonely cottage Synge frequently stayed in, and (below) his signature appears in the cottage visitors' book.*

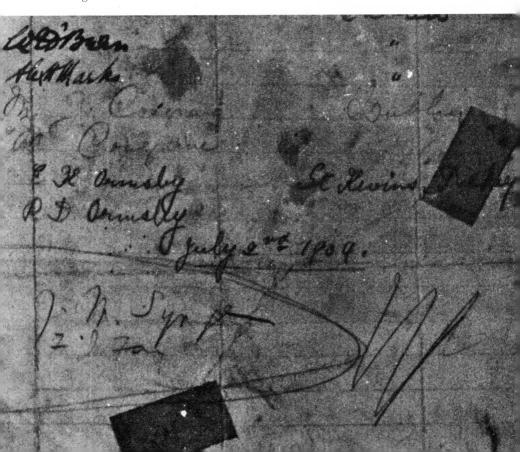

the ewes from the remoter slopes. In the villages the low-ceilinged public houses offered him companionship and porter, lamplit havens where the seats were bags of flour and pipe tobacco mingled with the smell of great flitches of bacon. Glenmalure and a story heard on the Aran Islands provided the material for *In the Shadow of the Glen*, Glenmacnass the setting for a poem. And the talk of tinkers and the remembrances of old men filled his notebooks, for, as he himself has said: 'Where the imagination of the people, and the language they use, is rich and living, it is possible for a writer to be rich and copious in his words, and at the same time to give the reality, which is the root of all poetry, in a comprehensive and natural form'.

He found it in abundance not only in Wicklow, but from herds and fishermen along the coast from Kerry to Mayo and from beggar-women and ballad singers around Dublin.

3

Wicklow, so rich in natural beauty, offers little in the way of fine buildings. Frank O'Connor, who had always a tendency to go on a bit on the subject of architecture, mentions only four: Avondale, a Regency house on the Rathdrum-Arklow road, which I found remarkable only for the fact that it was Charles Stewart Parnell's home; Tinnehinch, outside Enniskerry, given by the nation to Henry Grattan and almost taken away altogether from the nation since by time, aided and abetted by official neglect; Russborough, on the road to Poulaphouca, in West Wicklow, which was built in 1748 and looks wonderful from the roadway (O'Connor describes it as the most beautiful of all the Irish country houses); and Powerscourt House, designed by the same architect, which is odd in being ponderous and plain in the front, and strikingly beautiful at the rear, where wide steps lead down to fountains and terraced gardens which are dominated by distant mountains, Sugar Loaf in its characteristic way lording it over them all. I would say it is like something you would find painted on a Japanese fan, were it not an insult to describe any part of Wicklow other than in terms of itself.

The estate got its name from Eustace le Poer who had a castle on the site during the reign of Edward I, but lost it to the O'Tooles, Irish lords of Wicklow. It was granted to Sir Richard Wingfield by Queen Elizabeth and the grant was confirmed by James I. The present house dates back to about 1730, but the large reception hall was built for the visit of George IV in 1821, who arrived, according to popular report, the worse for drink. The platform which was erected specially so that His Majesty might have a grand stand view of the estate's 400 foot waterfall was washed away overnight by a sudden torrent, much to the disappointment of His Majesty and, it is said, of some of his disaffected subjects, who wished it had waited until he was on it. J. B. Malone in his book *Walking in Wicklow* tells another story of the visit. There was much talk at the time of the gold that had been found in one of the rivers and the local gold rush it led to. When one of the larger nuggets was shown to George IV during his visit, he examined it with interest, then absentmindedly slipped it into his waistcoat pocket 'while Court etiquette forbade the disconsolate owner to ask his treasure back'.

The terraces and gardens were designed some thirty years after the royal visit by an eccentric genius called Daniel Robertson. A martyr to gout, he supervised the work while sitting in a wheelbarrow grasping a bottle of sherry. When the bottle was empty he called it a day and ordered the workmen to wheel him back to the house. The work continued through the years of the Great Famine, providing merciful relief for about a hundred labourers and their families. When it was completed the gates, the statuary and the fountains were added from time to time, mainly from European sources.

The main avenue of the estate follows the course of the Dargle river for about three miles, by open parkland at first, then through wooded lands smelling of wild garlic, then to the waterfall in the Deer Park at its southern extremity, where the slopes of Djouce and Maulin mountains join each other to form a precipitous barrier. Beyond lie the wild territories of the O'Byrnes and the O'Tooles, whose dispossessed chieftains kept the lords of Powerscourt and even the rulers of Dublin from easy sleep for hundreds of years. The gardens are open to the public during the Summer season.

Long before Synge searched the glens of Wicklow for a truth to live by, the monks of St. Kevin sought Christ in the solitude of Glendalough. Kevin came first, a hermit monk of the 6th century who wanted only an anchorite's retreat and the company of God. But his holiness attracted followers, and his followers attracted students and scholars and eventually what began as a hermit's cell became a monastic city, to be made rich by gifts and the industry of the monks and so a coveted prize in the eyes of kings and marauders, whose capacity for contemplation began and ended with the possibility of easy plunder. Yet Glendalough, before it attained the material importance which robbed it of its right to be left alone, became one of the great centres of learning of the Irish Church, which attracted scholars from far and wide and later sent them abroad again to spread their learning to Britain and the Courts of European kings. From its founding in the 6th century to its final destruction by the forces of Richard II at the end of the fourteenth century Glendalough, in addition to the natural calamities of flood and famine, suffered plunder and burning at the hands of the Danes, the Normans and the native Irish themselves. It produced one Archbishop of Dublin and Prime Archbishop of Armagh in Laurence O'Toole, a scion of the Clan O'Toole, Chiefs of Wicklow, so the secular power eventually controlled at Glendalough, as it did elsewhere, mainly because to the Irish way of thinking everything in the tribal territory belonged of right to the tribe—and that included the church, which ought to be ruled by an Abbot of the blood. Laurence was an O'Toole whose mother was of the O'Byrnes, both powerful Wicklow families, while his sister was married to Diarmuid MacMorrough, notorious in Irish history for having invited the Normans to invade Ireland. Eva, who married the principal commander of the Norman forces, Strongbow (immediately

(Opposite) . . . *only resignation and acceptance persist, in the turn of phrase, the set of the features, a tone in the voice or the inherited gesture of the hands.*

D. Rooney & Son Funeral undertakers

after the sack of Waterford, it is said, among the corpses and the ruins) was a niece of Laurence. The Archbishop, however, remained on the side of his own people, the O'Tooles and the O'Byrnes, until his death in 1180, despite the capture of Dublin and the sacking of Glendalough.

To-day all that remains are the ancient city gate, a round tower built probably in the ninth century which is perfectly preserved, numerous small churches, some with Romanesque carvings, and a wealth of legends and superstitions which in Ireland are the natural accretions of antiquity.

One of these concerns the workmen who were engaged in building the Cathedral. Their hours were governed by the maxim: To rise with the lark and lie down with the lamb. After a few weeks St. Kevin, inspecting the work, noticed they were all looking exhausted and asked them what was wrong. They explained to him that they were fulfilling their bargain to rise with the lark, but that the larks of Glendalough got up so early in the morning that they were worn out. So the Saint prayed to God to restrain the larks and God took pity and did so. From that day to this, local tradition says, larksong has never been heard over Glendalough. The legend inspired Thomas Moore to write a poem with an opening which must surely be one of the worst in the world:

> By that lake whose gloomy shore
> *Skylark never warbles o'er*

The poem goes on to relate another legend about a beautiful lady called Kathleen, who, in all piety, went to listen to the Saint preaching. Unfortunately, 'unholy thoughts crept in amidst the telling of her beads, and she became enamoured of the youthful saint'. She visited him so frequently at his first retreat near Lough Tay that he left it and found refuge in a cave in the cliff face above Glendalough's upper lake. Here he was safe for a time, until one day, while Kathleen was wandering disconsolately among the fields, Kevin's favourite dog ran up to her. When she had played with him for a while he turned and ran off

Powerscourt Waterfall (opposite). *The platform, which was erected so that his Majesty might have a grandstand view of the estate's 400 foot waterfall, was washed away overnight by a sudden torrent.*

again. Kathleen followed and was led to the saint's cave. Kevin, wakened out of his sleep by her bending form became so angry that he pushed her over the cliff to her watery grave.

As an example of what I have called the Honour-and-Virtue school of thought which at one time frustrated any attempts to see Irish history in terms of humanity or humour, two sensible and scholarly men went to some pains to prove that Kevin did not kill Kathleen at all:

> 'As a gross calumny has been committed to the durability of type and rendered celebrated by the verse of the last bard and historian of Ireland (poor Tom Moore) it devolves upon us as a duty to vindicate the saint's character from so foul an imputation as that of murdering a lady who was in love with him. The saint had no wish to kill the girl . . . and the occurrence took place, not at Glendalough, but at the monastery of St. Lochanus . . . '

All this solemn nonsense about something which no sane person could take seriously is typical of a patriotism which had gone a little bit mad. It was unable (unlike Synge's Pegeen Mike) to understand the great gap between a gallous story and a dirty deed.

I was helped into that cave as a young child. The memory of it is fragmentary and ill-lit, for I must have been only four or five years old, but it persists. Whenever I look across the upper lake at the steep cliff of Lugduff Mountain I remember the ripple of oars in the water, then the cliff face looming above, a sense of fright and excitement, then one hand pushing my bottom and hands above yanking me into the stony hollow. It stands, perpendicularly, about twenty-five feet above water level and has been tattooed inside with the names or initials of hundreds of visitors. The Reverend Caesar Otway, who climbed into it himself in his time, noted some illustrious ones:

> 'Amongst the many, I could observe those of Sir Walter Scott, Lord Combermere; and of certain blue-stocking dames, as, for instance, Lady Morgan, who made it her temporary *boudoir*.'

He himself wasn't above scratching the letters C.O. where he thought the shoulder of the saint may have rested.

Sir Walter Scott paid his visit in 1825. Although in declining health at the time, he satisfied honour by climbing into the bed. When Scott had left, Lord Plunkett explained to the guide that he was a poet.

'Poet', said she, 'divil the bit of him, but an honourable gentleman;—he gave me half-a-crown!'

Another poet, Austin Clarke, who had a strict Victorian upbringing, recorded his own first visit to this remnant of 7th century Ireland:

> 'I saw Glendalough for the first time when I was a child and my memory of it is still alert; beyond the Round Tower and the Seven Churches, on the edge of the green between the two lakes, were all sorts of wagonettes, brakes, jaunting cars; a great crowd was dancing, singing, while strong men staggered about in the sunshine, clutching bottles of porter or whiskey. So for the first time I became aware of merry Ireland, the Ireland of race-meetings, bank holidays, and late home-comings!'

Luxury coaches and private cars have replaced the brakes and the wagonettes and spill out more visitors than ever to Kevin's holy city. They try to span the stump of the old cross with their arms to get a wish; they have their photographs taken, they visit the Deer Stone for luck, eat their sandwiches, buy their souvenirs. Yet Glendalough retains a unique peace which even their transistors never really shatter.

When they go home and evening settles it is possible to absorb it fully. Then is the time to search the graveyard for the out of the way things few of them ever take the trouble to find; odd inscriptions, or examples of the work of a local mason called Cullen, whose eccentricity it was to decorate his gravestones with scenes from the Passion in which Roman soldiers, accompanying Christ to His Crucifixion, are dressed in cocked hats and eighteenth century costume and carry guns.

Or to cross the stream by the Deer Stone and walk the shores of the lake, while the serenity and silence woo the mind back to an age when scholars laboured at all times, by sunlight and candlelight, to lift their earth a little nearer to paradise, or persuade God to bend down His Presence to man. The Tower still points in the direction of their thoughts, the ruined churches cluster in the long grasses, the two bright lakes in the valley reflect the hues of that heaven they mortified the living flesh to merit. Their bones have rested through long centuries all around, awaiting the deliverance of Judgement Day. When it comes, I have a fancy, they will waken out of slumber, not to the stern blast of Gabriel's trumpet, but to the trilling of thousands of larks from whom God, at last, has lifted his Divine ban.

5

Beyond Glendalough lies Glenmalure, perhaps the remotest glen of all. For those who don't draw back from rough going and heavy climbing it is possible to go directly by the remains of an old route from Glendalough, over the shoulder of Derrybaun mountain, past Refeart Church and St. Kevin's original hermitage, which was there before the monastic city was begun. The more orthodox way nowadays is by the military road from Laragh to Drumgoff, where the usual abandoned barracks reminds one of redcoats and the uprising of 1798.

To the right is the entrance to the glen, which is marked by a huge boulder inscribed to the memory of two leaders separated in time by two centuries of history:

An gleann in ar bhris Fiach Ó Broin cath ar Ghallaibh 1580 A.D.
(The Glen in which Fiach (McHugh) O'Byrne defeated the English 1580 A.D.)

Sa ghleann so do bhí a longphort ag Micheál Ó Duibhir agus a chuid laocra 1798 A.D.
(Michael Dwyer and his men had their headquarters in this glen 1798 A.D.)

These remote fastnesses of Wicklow have provided shelter for the defeated and the dispossessed in every century of Irish history. Fiach McHugh O'Byrne ruled it in the time of Queen Elizabeth and so defied the writ of her royal highness that in

1551 she thought fit to remind her Lord Deputy, Sir James Crofts, of his business:

'Above all things, to reduce the O'Byrnes and the O'Tooles in their country'.

By 1580, some thirty years or so later, there was little sign of improvement and Lord Grey was furnished with the same instructions. The Queen, very understandably, was growing impatient and Lord Grey, equally understandably, was concerned to keep his head, which he needed for his plumed hat. He made a hasty march to engage O'Byrne without giving soldierly consideration to the kind of terrain he was to give battle in, and his defeat, which the stone commemorates, was the result.

Another of Elizabeth's enemies, Red Hugh O'Donnell, Prince of Donegal, escaped from Dublin Castle, crossed the hills in a snowstorm, and found refuge here with O'Byrne's people. That was eleven years later, on Christmas Night 1591, under yet another Governor, Sir John Perrott. Governors, it will be seen, tended to come and go. When Fiach McHugh finally made submission it was to an ancestor of the Lords of Powerscourt, a Captain Richard Wingfield, who was knighted as a reward.

The huge rock which soars above the commemorative boulder is worth climbing for its wide view of the valley. Michael Dwyer the 1798 leader, used it as a look-out point. It dominates the barracks, where nothing much could go on without his guerrilla band being aware of it. At the farthest end of the glen, just across the river, the ruins of a cottage are another reminder of Dwyer. A woman lived there who had the habit now and then, of coming out on to the roadway in front to comb her hair. If she did so, the look-out post high up the mountain knew the military were up to something and took precautions.

Memories of 1798 and the exploits of Dwyer and other heroes have become part of folklore, not only here in Glenmalure, but in the countryside around Lough Tay and the Devil's Glen, in Baltinglass and Rathdrum, in the Glen of Imaal where Dwyer's cottage can still be visited; and Kilranalagh Churchyard, to which the young rebel MacAllister's body was moved by Anne Devlin and her friends under the eyes of the yeomenry, so that he might rest there with his executed comrades, and not be lonely in the old churchyard of Leitrim where he had been first interred. The young girls of the neighbourhood (she tells us) decorated the graves with garlands and ribbons and silks.

All that is past now, the terror of 1798, with its floggings and hangings and the feats of the O'Byrnes and the O'Tooles, who rallied from their crags and their bogs to challenge Elizabeth. Yet something persists, in ballad, in landscape itself, in a tenacious and stubborn pride.

In Glencree, at the very beginning of the century, in a remote, rock strewn clearing up the mountainside known as the Raven's Glen, an old man lived on his own in a shack which he had thrown together himself. He had nothing in this world but a few mountain ewes, which he brought down to market perhaps a couple of times a year. Whenever he did so he spent his share of the sale on drink just like everyone else. When the drink worked in him it stirred up a deep bitterness, a sense of wrong which, when the pubs had closed, sent him marching up the long avenue of stately trees to Powerscourt House. When he reached the door he used to lift up his ashplant and hammer on it with a noise like thunder, shouting:

'Leave my house, youse usurpers and imposters'.

He would keep this up until the police came to take him away. Next day he would be brought before the R.M. who was, of course, Lord Powerscourt himself. His Lordship would hear the matter solemnly, fine the old man a shilling, bind him to take the pledge (which wasn't much trouble to a man returning to the inhospitable solitudes of the Raven's Glen) and wait until the next Fair the old man would attend, in the fairly certain belief that what never failed to happen before is pretty certain to happen again. It always did.

That old man's name was O'Toole. And the people of Glencree, who quite understood the situation, always referred to him as The King O'Toole. It is a story which, in its own odd way, throws a tiny light into the labyrinthine tenacities of the Irish soul.

4

Rock of Ages

VIEWED from the top of the Rock of Cashel, County
Tipperary is magnificent. Under a wide sky of changing
landscapes the blue shapes of mountains—Slievenamon,
The Knockmealdowns, the Comeraghs and the Galtees—rise
from the plains of the Golden Vale, those broad and fertile acres
which once supported a long dynasty of Munster kings and
were seized in turn by Norman and Cromwellian settler. The
roads all around are peaceful to travel, with a slow air about
their heavily grown hedges, their narrow bridges and occasional
cottages. Neither roads nor people have much show of hurry
on them in Tipperary: there is always time to stare over a gate
at the growing crops, or to lean on a bridge looking down at the
reeds and the fish. In sunshine the colours lift the heart, especially when there is just enough cloud moving lazily above to
make subtle changes of tone as the shadows travel across the
great width of landscape. The towns, almost all of them, have
an individual character. Carrick-on-Suir, which has an Elizabethan mansion on the wooded banks of the river, is peaceful
and reflective. It is said to have been built specially by one of the
Dukes of Ormond in anticipation of a visit from Queen
Elizabeth, but she seems to have changed her mind. The town
of Fethard, where there are the ruins of an Augustinian foundation and some interesting carvings, including a Síle-na-gig,
feels always as though its thoughts are fixed on some heavy

tragedy of the past. I am not aware that it has suffered any more or less than the rest, but there is something dark and brooding in the atmosphere. Cahir has a busy air. Being on the main Dublin to Cork route it has its share of traffic, yet there is still a place for the donkey drawn cart and its couple of milk churns for the creamery. One shopkeeper displays farmers' boots and heavy-wearing shirts by pinning them to the telegraph pole outside, where they flap and dangle in the wind almost from bottom to top.

Tipperary's Rock of Cashel is, without question, one of the most spectacular sights in Ireland. It is also, I have found, one of the most incomprehensible. Although I have been there in the company of a number of knowledgeable people, including Frank O'Connor, who collected Irish monasteries and their complicated history the way others collect stamps, I am still unable to arrive at a serviceable account of its meaning.

A huge outcrop of limestone rock, it raises its bewildering conglomeration of churches and crosses more than two hundred feet above the modest town which shelters beneath it. Tradition claims it was once the dwellingplace of the immortals, people of the Tuatha De Danaan, a race of sorcerers and magicians who could make themselves invisible at will, and the circumstances of its discovery by the men of Munster are set out in Cormac's Glossary:

'Corc son of Lugaid was in Cathair Etain Tarb and Temair Eimen, which are side by side, when Cashel was revealed to Durdriu, swineherd to the king of Ely, and Cuiriran, swineherd to the king of Muskerry. It was they who first discovered Cashel, and the woods of Cashel were yellow at the time, and the mast was plentiful there'.

That was near the end of the fourth century. The kings of Munster had their seat at Cashel from then until the end of the eleventh century. By this time Cork had become the capital of South Munster and Limerick of North Munster, so Murtagh O'Brien, finding he needed Cashel no longer, gave it outright to the Church in 1101, a gesture without precedent in Irish law, which regarded land as the inalienable property of the clan,

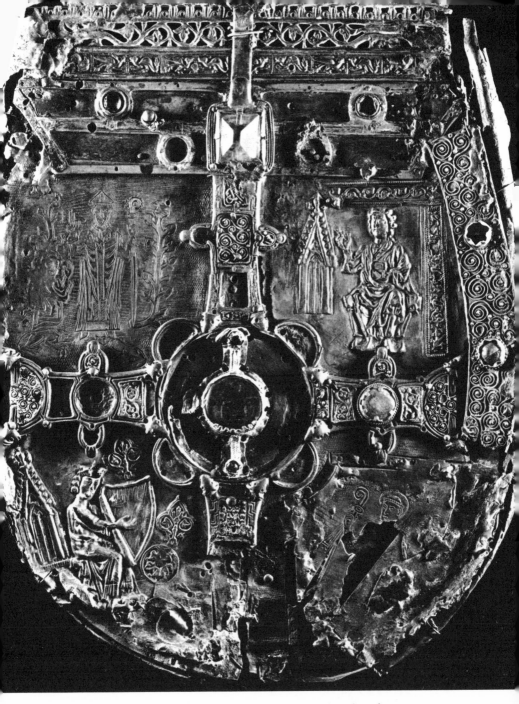

St. Patrick's Tooth. *St. Patrick has always been a source of pride and complacency.*

not of any individual. In this case his decision was condoned and Cashel began its growth as a great ecclesiastical centre. It fell on lean days with the impact of the Reformation at the end of the sixteenth century. In the next century the townspeople took refuge in the Cathedral but were murdered there (3,000 of them) by the Cromwellian army, who proceeded to wreck the great crucifix and the sacred images. In 1749 Archbishop Agar stripped the Cathedral of its roof—and that was the end.

The buildings include Cormac's Chapel, the Cathedral, the Castle, the Hall of the Vicars Choral and the Round Tower. Cormac's chapel is regarded as a purely Irish building. It is not fortified, unlike the Cathedral, which shows the Continental influence and incorporates a castle at its west end. The difference (as Stephen Gwynn points out) embodied a lesson which the Irish kings failed to take note of: the need to protect their key places with strong fortifications and indeed, the greater need to weld together their numerous small states, with their shifting alliances, under a strong central power. When the Normans came some thirty years later, that failure was to prove fatal.

In the course of a script for a Bird's Eye View (BBC) film on Ireland, I remarked that it was at Cashel St. Patrick is said to have plucked the three-leaved shamrock from the ground to demonstrate the mystery of the Trinity—three Gods in One. I had an angry letter from a woman (probably a Meath woman) who was positive the incident took place at Tara. When I asked a friend his opinion he re-opened a controversy I thought decently buried.

'Which St. Patrick?' he asked.

Legend has not the truth of fact. It can become true, nevertheless, by being absorbed so deeply into the race consciousness that it is made to occur by some mysterious, retrospective projection. By general agreement, Ireland has decided that Patrick plucked the shamrock. Whether it is a fact or not does not greatly matter to the true Irishman; it is a traditionally held truth and therefore far more solid and indisputable than a mere fact and capable, because of its insubstantial nature, of taking place at Tara or at Cashel or at both, or indeed any number of places provided local tradition has sanctioned it.

St. Patrick has always been a source of pride and complacency, a man of recognisable character, as unquestionably *there* as the rock of Cashel itself. He had landed in Ireland in 432, with instructions from Pope Celestine to convert the nation and banish the druids. He preached to the kings and plucked the shamrock from the sod at his feet to drive his point home. The matter having been settled in that fashion, the people queued in thousands to be baptised and every second newborn male was christened Patrick. The shamrock became the national emblem. It was a distinction to be Paddy The Irishman.

I can still recall the great scandal of 1942, when a book called *The Two Patricks* was published by a learned Irish professor who advanced the theory that there was one Patrick (Palladius Patrick) whose mission lasted from 432–461, and another who arrived in 462 and died about 490. The suggestion caused a national upheaval. If the careers of the two Patricks, through scholarly bungling, had become inextricably entangled, who did what? And worse still—which of them was the Patron Saint? If you addressed a prayer to one, might it not be delivered by mistake to the other? There was a feeling abroad that any concession to the two Patricks theory would lead unfailingly to a theory of no Patrick at all. Fortunately another book on St. Patrick has been published since. It is a difficult work to follow, one which gives the general reader the feeling of having barged uninvited into the company of a score of argumentative scholars, none of whom ever lifts his head to acknowledge the same general reader's presence as they continue a debate which was begun before he came in and will continue long after he has given up and left, but it scotched the attempt to make a double gentleman out of the Patron Saint. In fact, R. P. C. Hanson, who wrote it, confirmed the missionary dates followed by teaching and tradition. The Irish view of Patrick's rugged but lovable character and the fundamental story of his career, remained unchanged. He was taken as a slave to Ireland by Irish raiders while still a youth and he herded flocks in sun and rain on the slopes of Sliabh Mis. He escaped at last to his home but returned to bring Christianity to the Irish, after a dream in which the people cried out to him: 'We beg you, holy youth, come and

97

work once more among us'.

For the rest, Hanson denies that Pope Celestine had any interest in the conversion of the Gael living at the butt end of a barbarous world, or that Patrick was prepared for his mission through study at Lerins or Auxerre, a conclusion based on the fact that Patrick's Latin was deplorable. Patrick thought so himself. It was a perpetual source of embarrassment to him, so much so that he felt it necessary to apologise to the Rhetoricians for his inability to master their art. He might not have worried. If the object of the scholarly art of rhetoric was to persuade, then he had them ignominiously outclassed. Ireland's response to the Christian message is a phenomenon of history.

The druids had prophesied Patrick's coming with little welcome for a gospeller of novelties who was going to smash their idols and drive them out of business.

> Bare poll will come over the wild sea
> His mantle hole-headed, his staff crook-headed
> His altar in the east of his house
> And all his people answering Amen, amen.

It had no effect. Ireland took to the Christian message with an enthusiasm which involved not only itself, but the rest of Europe. Soon the little monasteries were springing up in every quarter, the saintly bands were sailing the seas in their little skin-covered boats, off to spread the tidings to all reachable corners of the earth, or to search for a remote and blessed isle at the edge of the world untouched by original sin, where they could build their cells and practise virtuous austerities perpetually.

Their asceticism matched their zeal. Fasting on one meal of vegetables and herbs a day, their sleep broken for prayer at regulated hours, their punishments for inattention or omission

St. Patrick's Day Parade (opposite). *There was a feeling that any concession to the two Patricks theory would lead unfailingly to a theory of no Patrick at all.*

rigidly laid down, they strove to dismiss self and punish the flesh so that sin would become impossible. St. Kevin of Glendalough, it is said, prayed for so long with his arms outstretched that a bird nested in one of his palms. St. Ailbe made himself a cross of stones out-of-doors and stretched himself on it to recite the psalter every day at daybreak, regardless of the weather. Others prayed standing in icy water. If much of this is legend, there is nothing fictional about the Rule or the Penitentials, which required in some cases 'three hundred prostrations every day, and three at every canonical hour'. The scourge was much in use: up to two hundred blows (twenty-five at a time) for serious offence with, at the other end of the scale, six blows for not shaving before serving at Mass. There was even a punishment for singing out of tune. Yet the monasteries overflowed. Latin culture and learning took root in Ireland at a moment when the collapse of the Roman Empire, the outpouring of the barbarians and the destruction of order and communication were threatening their extinction in civilized Europe. These monks were to play an important part in preserving and restoring what was going under; from the fifth to the ninth century, when the Danish raids interrupted monastic development, they acted an important part as guardians of the Christian tradition.

To-day the remnants of the monastic movement lie scattered all over Ireland, from its little 6th century beginnings in lake islands on the Shannon to its absorption and replacement by the Norman conquerors in the Abbeys of Ennis and Golden (Co. Tipperary) and other places. I have a memory of Frank O'Connor surveying the surroundings from the tower of Jerpoint Abbey and remarking with an obvious sense of its impressiveness and its ordered surroundings: 'Ah, Chaucer country'.

Perhaps I have less love of order, or of well fenced land, or for that matter, the extremes of culture, though I acknowledge grandeur in architecture, and what is usually described as soaring splendour. For me the charm and indeed the heartbreak, of what the monastic movement has to say lie in the smaller buildings of earlier centuries, those at Clonmacnoise certainly, but especially in what remains among the wilds of the Dingle Peninsula, on the lake islands of the River Shannon, in the unbelievable isolation of Skellig Michael.

I had my first sight of Skellig from a helicopter when I was scripting the Bird's Eye View film. It was one of those few occasions when I felt I not only looked on something unique but, by some trick of angle and light perhaps, something which had revealed to me the essence of a civilisation. We had come from Shannon airport, down the mouth of the river for a while, then over the towns of Listowel and Tralee. In cold March weather, with thick clumps of mist whirling between us and its high desert of bogland and rock, we crossed Brandon's holy mountain, where the hermits had built their solitary huts over a thousand years before. Beyond that, nine miles from the nearest point of the mainland, often inaccessible even to-day in its waste of grey, heaving waters, rose Skellig Michael. It soared precipitously out of the ocean to a height of more than seven hundred feet, ending in a shaft of rock that was more a jagged spire than a summit, with gannets scattering from its recesses like a thick cloud of blown snow. When they had cleared we could see below us the layout of the monastic settlement; the two small churches, the oratories, the beehive dwellings, the burial enclosures, the stonestepped roadway they had cut out of the face of the rock. It was like some primitive carving hewn above the sea. If God was nearest where the world ends, here, surely, was God.

I think of the carvings on Muireadach's cross at Monasterboice, how close they are, in style as in concept, to the simple religious certainties of childhood. In one weathered panel Eve tempts Adam, or Abel is murdered; in another God sits on Judgment Day above the demons and the damned, the saved on His Right Hand, the wicked on His left. In a panel below, a soul sits in an entirely practical looking weighing scales where his good actions are balanced against his bad.

For the monks of Skellig Michael it was hardly different. Heaven was above, Hell was below. The stars were lit at night by angels and quenched at dawn. The winds tearing at the rock and the seas when they sought to devour it were moved by demons. If prayer was potent, so were charms and spells. The soul contended now with the devil and his legions, now with the hosts of witchery:

> I have set around me all these powers
> Against every hostile savage power
> Directed against my body and my soul,
> Against the incantations of false prophets
> Against the black laws of heathenism
> Against the false laws of heresy
> Against the deceits of idolatry
> Against the spells of women and smiths and druids
> Against all knowledge that blinds the soul of man.

As in a child's world too, wonders were next door neighbours. If a holy man wished to travel by sea, a stone boat floated him safely to his destination. When a voyaging saint wished to say Mass, God provided a whale and the good man, taking it for an island, said Mass on its back. Saint Ciaran travelled with a tame fox to carry his psalter, and a deer who bent down its antlers to provide a lectern for his study book. St. Brigid, when the day was warm, hung her cloak on a sunbeam. Colman the hermit of Sliabh Corann had three friends in the world: a cock to crow out at the times of prayer, a mouse to waken him from sleep at the fifth hour, a fly who followed the lines of the book as he read and, if he were interrupted, marked the place he had stopped at until he came back.

In the medieval world the miracles and the magic are endless, and nowhere more so than Ireland. Yet side by side with the spells and charms, the demonic conspiracies and the angelic visitors (who, as Fr. Ryan S.J. has remarked, seem to have been on hand for consultation in all perplexities) the brethren toiled painfully and fruitfully in the cause of learning and truth. Work in the monastery's scriptorium went on ceaselessly as the monks copied texts and made books either for their students' instruction, or to be packed in leather bags which the missionaries would carry on their backs in their journeys through Europe. There is a vivid picture in *Old Ireland, her Scribes and Scholars* (Robert E. McNally S.J.):

Muireadach's Cross...*a soul sits in an entirely practical looking weighing scales.*

'The scribe worked a large portion of the day hunched over a slanting desk with his bare feet on the cold, stone floor. With goose quill in his first three fingers, he spent the long hours tracing the so-called Irish letters in jet ink on well polished white parchment or vellum. The equipment for executing these precious works of art was simple indeed—a supply of well sharpened quills, pigments for producing red, yellow, blue and green, a sharp blade or pumice stone for correcting the text, sand for drying ink and a keen edged knife for sharpening the pens. From every point of view scribal work was difficult. It was ordinarily done in silence, frequently in hunger, invariably in discomfort. The scriptorium was poorly lighted; and on wintry days, the cold freely penetrated and benumbed the body of the scribe.'

Sometimes the scribes got relief from the drudgery by scribbling personal comments in the margin. One book, Priscian's *Institutio de Arte Grammatica* has a marginal notation in Irish—'*Alas—my hand!*' followed later by '*O my breast, Holy Virgin*'. A few pages further on the scribe is more cheerful and writes: '*It is time for dinner*'.

So, on the edge of Europe, in these buildings which are now in ruins, a thousand hands laboured to save a culture from obliteration. There were quite chatty marginal notes too: '*Wonderful is the robin there singing to us. And our cat has escaped from us.*'

2

Of the early lake island monasteries Inis Cealtra (or Holy Island) in Lough Derg, County Clare, is easily accessible. It lies less than half a mile from the mainland at its nearest point, the route still taken by the funerals of those from the mainland who still exercise their right to burial in its holy ground. From Mountshannon, where a boat can be hired, the journey is a little over a mile. Wooded around its shores, with an easy landing platform, it contains the remains of a settlement founded originally by St. Caimin in the seventh century. Apart from the churches and the Round Tower, it has a structure called the Confessional, so constricted inside that a man could neither sit nor stand. It was probably built that way as a penitential. The Saints' graveyard has numerous carved gravestones, many of them so overgrown with a carpet of moss that I remember spending the idle hours of a summer afternoon cleaning some of them. Whether that was the right thing to do after all I don't know. The ones I cleaned seemed better preserved from the elements than the ones already exposed. There is a church called 'The Church of the Wounded Men' (Teampall na bhFear nGonta). Who they were no one knows. When King Guaire of Connaught visited Inis Cealtra with Cuimin of Clonfert he

Race Card Seller by Jack B. Yeats ... *the three card trick man is happy to lose, but happier still to win.*

was asked what he would wish to see the Church filled with:

'With gold and silver', said the king, 'but not for greed. Rather for my soul's sake to give it to the saints and their Churches and the poor of the world'.

Caimin, the hermit, said he would wish it filled with misery and disease 'that I might suffer them all in my own body'.

Cuimin, the scholar, wished differently again. 'I'd wish it piled up with books', he said, 'so that students might study them and spread God's word in the ears of every man'. All three had their wish, according to the old text. Later the Danes came. It helped with the misery and the suffering, but did no good to the gold and the books.

About thirty miles up river from Inis Cealtra, on the east bank of the Shannon, St. Ciaran founded a monastery in 548 A.D. which grew eventually into the great monastic city of Clonmacnoise. The remains to-day are extensive and, apart from the nine churches, include two Round Towers, five High Crosses and over five hundred early gravestones. Its fame as a graveyard was such that it was believed that no soul buried there could ever be damned.

932 A prayer for Uallach
UALLACH, INGEN MUIMHNECHAIN,
BANECCLES ERENN, D'ECC
(Uallach, daughter of Muimhnechain, Abbess of Ireland, died.)

1079 A prayer for Mael Chiarain
MAEL CHIARAIN, MAC CUINN NA MBOCHT,
COMHARBA CIARAIN, D'ECC. BA EISEDHEN
ORDAN OCUS AIRMITTIN CHLUANNA INA
REMHES.
(Mael Chiarain, son of Conn the Almoner, Abbot of Clonmacnoise, died. He was the glory and admiration of Clonmacnoise in his reign.)

As in many other cases, what began as a centre of holiness and learning grew rich on gifts and the industry and craftsmanship of the monks. Clonmacnoise became a city with little streets of wooden houses, craftsmen's workshops, and paved roadways. The remains of one of these, the Pilgrims Road, laid down in 1070, survives to-day. Inevitably its wealth attracted plunderers, both native and Norse. When Thorgestr and his warriors occupied Clonmacnoise his wife Ota added to the desecration by giving heathen oracles from its high altar. In the twelfth century, a thief looted the Cathedral and got away with, among other items: 'A model of Solomon's Temple, a silver goblet, a silver cup with a gold cross, a gold drinking horn, the drinking horn of O Riada, King of Aradh; a silver chalice with gold plating, and a design by the daughter of Rory O'Connor (the last High King of Ireland)'. A thousand years after its foundation, the English from Athlone completed the destruction of Clonmacnoise, leaving 'not a bell, large or small, nor a statue, nor an altar, nor a book nor a jewel, not even the glass in a window'.

In Lough Ree, further north still, there are at least two settlements, Inisbofin and Inis Cleraun. To visit them in fine weather is, in any case, a pleasant and rewarding day's sailing from Athlone, but to make the journey in Frank O'Connor's company was to have a man who, in addition to his engagement with their history and architecture, had devoted much of his natural scholarship and skill to the translation of those poems which the scribes sometimes composed in the margins of the books they were copying.

We needed a dinghy in tow to land on Inisbofin, where trees and tangled undergrowth make it necessary to beat a path from the shore level. The settlement was originally founded in the 6th century by St. Rioch, but was burned and plundered repeatedly from the 8th to the 11th century by both Danes and Munstermen. To-day the remains of two 13th century Churches are overgrown and (up to five years ago at any rate) utterly neglected. The trees have rooted close to the walls, grave slabs are lying around without protection, the plaque which warns that the buildings are in the care of the Department responsible for the safe keeping of Ancient Monuments has long since become entitled to that protection itself: it is still the British one.

Inis Cleraun is in the northern reaches of Lough Ree, just to the Longford side of the Roscommon-Longford border which divides the lake down the middle. The settlement was founded early in the 6th century by St. Diarmuid, the teacher of Ciaran of Clonmacnoise. Of the five churches built at different periods from then until the 12th century, the one which bears his name is best preserved.

Except for the cattle that graze among the ruins, the island is uninhabited. It is sheltered by trees and crossed by green trackways, and has the true island feeling of being open to wide skies and wide waters, a place full of light. The lake was warm to swim in on that calm summer afternoon. On shore unseen insects droned in chorus, as though the monks were still near at hand, reciting their litanies. As we left it behind, I asked Frank to recite his translation of one of the Hermit poems.

Grant me sweet Christ the grace to find—
Son of the living God—
A small hut in a lonesome spot
To make it my abode.

A little pool but very clear
To stand beside the place
Where all men's sins are washed away
By sanctifying grace.

A pleasant woodland all about
To shield it from the wind
And make a home for singing birds
Before it and behind.

A lovely Church, a home for God
Bedecked with linen fine
Where over the white gospel page
The Gospel candles shine.

My share of clothing and of food
From the King of fairest face
And I to sit at times alone
And pray in every place.

In the background, as his rich Cork tones gave out the verses, the water slapped against the bow and the rigging creaked in the evening breeze. It occurred to me that the waterway we were travelling was once the main road to the Continent for monks who were bent on pilgrimage to Rome and the Holy Land, or setting off for their missionary labours on the Continent, their books stowed away in their leather bags, the bread of Christ in its Chrismal, to be carried before them in the great forests to frighten off demons and wild beasts and robbers. They travelled far by land and sea, these early saints, encountering wonders, and witnessing miracles. Brendan, it was believed, had sailed to the very gates of Hell and on his way he found Judas chained to a rock in the midst of the ocean and treated him with compassion. Like children they were capable of believing practically anything, but like children also, they had innocence in abundance, so that their light and their faith still shine through remote centuries and their holiness lingers about the ruins of the little churches that once sheltered their ritual and their adoration.

5

A Word with the Barber

WHEN Dr. Johnson told Boswell the noblest prospect a Scotsman ever saw was the high road that led to England, it was a taunt which is paralleled in the Dublin man's attitude to the Corkman. There is a jaundiced Dublin belief that when a Corkman travels to Dublin for any occasion whatever, including a football final, he does so invariably on a one way ticket. And when the Corkmen have landed themselves the best jobs, they send right away for their nephews and cousins. It is a phenomenon, real or imaginary, which has kept the funny papers, the Pantomime comics and the public house cynics going since 1922—approximately. If it is beginning at long last to wane, I believe it is because a fairer spirit prevails and not (as is said) because Dublin audiences by now are made up almost entirely of Corkmen. Whatever the truth, it makes it difficult for a Dublin man like myself to say anything about Cork that has any hope of being accepted as unbiassed.

Except, of course, that it is a fine city. It began with a church and a school founded by St. Finbarr in the 6th century and, although both have long disappeared, the city has continued to grow about them ever since. The Danes wrested it from the native Irish, and the Normans took it from the Danes, but with good Cork Commonsense all three races intermarried and were absorbed into the Gaelic norm of living. Cork is as Irish as such a mixture can possibly be: which means it is very very Irish indeed. When I say it is a fine city I mean it, a city of noble bridges and buildings, a large harbour and quays which can accommodate transatlantic shipping at its very heart. There is a European look about its mixture of wide streets, steep hills, narrow laneways. Its centre lies in a hollow, so that at night its lights ring one around on all sides as in a giant amphitheatre. The last time I was there, just about a year ago, it looked light-hearted, even opulent, especially its young people in pubs and hotels. I don't mean the fur-coated, fat cigar kind of opulence. I mean the opulence of people who, whatever they have to spend on pleasure, spend it with good-mannered grace and enjoyment.

The citizens of Cork have certain characteristics. They speak with a rapidity which can leave a stranger in difficulties and they have the habit of expressing an opinion by canvassing yours. ('Do you think, like . . . ' they say, as a preface to laying down the law on some matter.) On the strength of their Opera House, they pride themselves on being a highly gifted musical people, which is not quite true. When they affect gentility, especially the women, they can be excruciating bores. I remember after a public recording session of the radio programme Question Time, a fur-coated woman, who spoke as though her mouth were full of pebbles, deplored the fact that one of the young men from the University had failed unexpectedly to answer a number of questions. 'Such a nice boy too', she concluded, 'and *so beautifully groomed*'.

Cork is better among its more common or garden elements, all of them enshrined in Frank O'Connor's early short stories; the pious, struggling mothers, the drinking men, the argumentative elect who regard themselves as intellectuals, the eccentrics, the amateur bandsmen who lower music and porter in equal measure. Cork to me, *is* Frank O'Connor. He was born and spent his early life there; lonely, obscure and practically penniless. By his own account his early education was hardly worth mentioning, yet in an environment that combined ignorance with hopelessness he longed for intellectual opportunity. He has said himself that the back lanes he grew up in were made bearable only because his gift of fantasy could banish them altogether for long stretches at a time. His father was an ex-British soldier with a disability pension, and the people of the narrow streets found it hard to understand how anyone who belonged to them should hanker after the unnecessary and probably dangerous luxury of an education. In those days the Rich were Rich, the poor were poor, and the British were in control anyway.

And so it might have remained, except that at this point Daniel Corkery, himself a writer and an artist, became the young O'Connor's schoolteacher. Corkery was also a fervent Nationalist, who wrote on the blackboard one day the first sentence in the Irish language that most of his class had ever seen. It said: 'Waken your courage, Ireland'.

It was a great embarrassment to the Headmaster, who felt it his duty to be the Crown's Own Henchman, but it inspired young Frank O'Connor. Corkery opened a window on the world he craved for, introducing him not only to literature and music and intellectual company but to the study of the Irish language and through it, to the cultural wealth of a hidden Ireland. It sent him cycling down remote country roads in search of an Irish past which still lingered in literature and stone. It was a search, not for a dead culture, but a living heritage, a birthright offering personal dignity and identity, which O'Connor found and claimed. Having learned Irish, O'Connor set out to teach it, visiting the people of the country cottages at an age when he was still young enough to absorb the experience creatively. It involved him also in the tragedy of the Civil War, in active service, in capture and imprisonment. Prison in turn provided time for study and reflection, which brought him to a typically dispassionate acceptance of the disastrous collapse of the republican ideal he had believed in. When he returned home after his release his mother, whom he adored, burst into tears and told him: 'It has made a man of you'. It had done something in addition. It had made a writer of him.

It is a truth of literature that nothing much happens to a writer after the age of twenty or so that will affect his work; the small store of material which informs the imagination for the rest of life is made up of the remembered experiences of childhood and youth. O'Connor was no exception. Memories of his father and mother, of the years of poverty, the characters and conversations of the laneways of Cork, the young people, the Troubles, these provide his best themes and he returns to them again and again. His interest in early Irish poetry, which he translated so finely, and his passion for monasteries and the remnants of the native way of life date also from his early youth.

How faithfully he had observed the characters of his Cork city was confirmed yet again the last time I was there. It was a filthy day of wind and torrential rain and I went to get a haircut. There was a middleaged customer in the chair, thin, carefully dressed, very sparse on top, a strict back-and-sides man. The walls of the shop were covered with theatre bills, signed photographs of concert stars and group pictures of brass bands and football teams. There was the usual smell of shaving soap and hair lotion. A discussion was going on on an ethical point concerning the suspension of a member of the Gaelic Athletic Association.

'And when was that?' asked the customer.

'Only the other week', said the Barber. 'Paddy O'Brien—a customer of mine'.

'The story, as I heard it', said the customer, 'is that he ran this social function which included old time waltzes and such like, which is contrary to the Association's ban on foreign dancing, as we both know'.

'That may be so', the barber agreed, 'but are you aware of the special circumstances?'

'And what were they?'

'This friend of Paddy's—a member of the G.A.A. too, died, the father of four young children. Paddy thought he'd do something to raise a little money like, something to tide the poor widow over. So he decided to organise a dance—which he did. The matter was reported to the Committee and Paddy was asked to explain himself. If he wanted to run a function, why wasn't it a Céilí'.

'A very proper question', said the customer severely, keeping an eye on the effects of the snipping scissors and lecturing his own image in the mirror at the same time.

'Paddy explained that the young people won't go to Céilís these days, not unless there's full and plenty of the modern stuff as well. There's no money in Céilís, if you follow me'.

'Quite irrelevant', said the customer, '*Rules are rules*'.

'That's what the Committee decision was. Didn't matter a damn what the circumstances, they said, it was foreign dancing and he was in breach of the rules. They suspended him for six months'.

'That was very proper. They did right—*according to their lights*'.

'Paddy was on the Committee himself', said the barber, 'but not wan iota of a difference did it make'.

'In my opinion', said the customer, 'it only makes it worse'.

The snipping at by now invisible hairs continued in silence. In the mirror the customer's face brooded. He rightly suspected the barber of sympathy with the suspended G.A.A. man. He disapproved. He was a man who would always be uncompromising in his condemnation of irregularity.

'Take a member of the Pioneer Total Abstinence Society', he began.

'Very well', said the barber, obligingly.

'If you and I know anything of the pioneers—which we do— they are one and all followers of the good Fr. Mathew whose statue adorns this city of ours, and they are sworn to abstain from intoxicating liquor and to discourage its use in others. You and I may judge that to be extreme, but there it is. Those are their *principles*'.

'I never had much time for that class of thinking', said the barber, 'what harm is there in a drink or two. Answer me that?'

'Quite irrelevant', said the customer. 'They have stated *a principle; they are members of a Society*. Suppose then, the friend of a Pioneer died and the widow is in want. The pioneer may decide to run a raffle. Perfectly in order. Nothing irregular as yet. But supposing the same pioneer decides to *raffle a bottle of whiskey*'.

The barber stopped snipping.

'How would you think he stands then', the customer concluded, '*In regard to the rules!*'

The barber was in no doubt whatever.

'You have a point there right enough', he conceded, 'a fair point. I wouldn't agree a pioneer has the right to raffle a bottle of whiskey—not for any purpose'.

'Of course you wouldn't', said the customer, 'because he's in breach of the rules. No—if he wants to do so, well and good: *but let him get out of the Pioneers*'.

When he had gone I took his chair.

'You heard all that, of course', said the barber.

'I couldn't help it', I answered.

'Well, let me tell you a bit more. Did you know I was in digs with a bus conductor this time, a man that wore a pioneer pin by day, and took it down at night. What would you think of that?'

'There's no principle in that', I said, taking the place of Mr. Upright and making as severe a face at the glass as I could muster.

'Well now', said the barber, 'there's more to it. The poor fellow had to do it—and I'll tell you why. He'd been disciplined so often for turning up to the job the worse for drink that the only way the Union could get him his job back was to make him join the Pioneers and take the pledge. I used to come across him every other night in the local, the pin in his pocket and him knocking back pints. I told him there was no principle in it and if he was a man at all to give up the jars or give up the job'.

'Very proper', I said.

'But no. I couldn't give up the jars, he said, and if I gave up the job where would I get the money for jars?'

I found nothing to say to that. The man may have been unprincipled, but he was a realist anyway. The barber felt the same. I knew it from the next piece of information he passed on.

'That crowd that suspended Paddy for running the dance', he said, 'the Committee men, moryah, the so-called G.A.A. vigilantes. I'll tell you what their principle is. Suspend poor Paddy for helping out a widow. And then home with themselves at the double to sit the night through, *glued to Telefís Éireann for the World Cup*'.

I left feeling I was materialising from the pages of one of Frank O'Connor's stories. Frank was a man who viewed the misadventures and conceits of mankind as essentially comic, and yet, in an odd way, as dignified. It was a mixture clearly evident in his own mature personality; in his veneration for Ireland's past and his mockery of what was ignoble in her present. He was a patriot who found it impossible over long periods to put up with life in Ireland (which is not at all unusual) and an iconoclast who spent his closing years campaigning to preserve the monuments of her civilisation from destruction — which is rather more so. If every anyone was bitterly wronged by the Honour-and-Virtue school, it was he.

2

A few miles to the north-west of Cork city lies Blarney and its famous Castle, where you kiss the Blarney Stone and are ever afterwards endowed with eloquence. Blarney (like Captain Boycott) has the distinction of having given a word to the English language through Queen Elizabeth's impatience with McCarthy, Baron of Blarney, who had an inexhaustible supply of answers and excuses for going his own sweet way instead of submitting to her Majesty's much reiterated commands.

'All Blarney', pronounced the Queen, when she received yet another polite enquiry after her health, accompanied by yet another reasonable explanation as to why McCarthy had not yet done what he kept on and on promising to do. A man with the gift of the Blarney is fair of word and soft of speech and, as they say, can swear a hole through an iron bucket.

The stone is set in the battlements, one hundred and twenty winding steps up from the ground. One legend says it was given to the McCarthys by Robert Bruce after the battle of Bannockburn; another that it was given to a Cormac McCarthy by a woman whom he rescued from drowning and who turned out to be a witch. The countryside around is well wooded and peaceful and much traversed by gaily coloured horse drawn caravans, with their complement of holiday makers who fancy a few weeks of Romany life. Their understanding of the practicalities

Frank O'Connor. *If ever anyone was bitterly wronged by the Honour-and-Virtue school, it was he.*

sometimes falls short. Two elderly English ladies returned
to base at the end of their week's touring holiday worn out.
They had enjoyed themselves very much they said, the weather
was perfect, but they had found it almost insuperably difficult
to get the horse into the caravan at night.

Kinsale is near at hand too. To-day it is largely an eighteenth
century town, grey houses clustering about a neck of blue
water, but in 1601 it witnessed a great national tragedy, when
Hugh O'Neill, Earl of Tyrone, was defeated after marching
from the other end of Ireland to relieve his besieged allies from
Spain. It was a defeat which led to the Flight of the Earls and the
collapse of the old Gaelic way of life. What it entailed for the
Great O'Neill, as he was called, will be worth some consideration later on.

West Cork and Kerry are such vast tourist regions that I
would have as much difficulty dealing with them properly as the
old ladies had with the horse. There are the usual pockets of
Shamroguery, Colleen Bawns and Shillelaghs, mixed in with
wild and breathtaking scenery and a great deal of the hidden
simplicities of Irish life. I remember hospitality and great courtesy from a woman who was making lace in a simple cottage in
the mountains above Glengarriff and good talk with shepherds,
who could simultaneously control the movements of their
sheep dogs which were gathering sheep on the bare mountain
slopes almost a mile away. Another time, walking from Killarney
to Dingle I got a lift from a man who turned out to be a descen-
dant of Daniel O'Connell. He had the Liberator's table in his
house, cracked in the middle where Dan had struck it a blow of
his fist. He had a Penal Cross too, one carved from bog oak, and
blackened with sweat from being hidden under the armpit of
the priest who carried it secretly. We got on together like a house
on fire until I praised Sean O'Faolain's biography of O'Connell
King of the Beggars. That did it. I was told the book was a
scandal and the author a thorough scoundrel, though I've re-
read that fine book since and can find no justification whatever
for the attack. I left the house in disgrace, met a lorry driver
who was headed for Listowel and never got to Dingle at all.

The next time I took the road to Dingle was by car, a trip

snatched in the few free hours between radio recordings, so that we had time only to look at Gallarus Oratory and call on Kruger Kavanagh, both of them famous Dingle institutions. The next was a visit with BBC producer Eddie Mirzoeff and a film crew. We set out from Castletownbere by helicopter, filmed here and there for some hours and were, from my amateur grasp of navigational matters, firmly in the middle of nowhere when the pilot asked me if there was any place near in which we could get morning coffee. I looked down. There was a great lump of uninhabited mountain below, forbidding cliffs ahead and the rolling sea beyond. The most I knew about our whereabouts was that we were certainly not over the Phoenix Park, but being the only Irishman at hand I had to pretend to be knowledgeable. Seawards, the nearest coffee shop would be in New York, so we turned inland. Stony fields, narrow tracks and an occasional cottage with hens and domestic animals scattering in all directions at the noise of our approach were the only signs of organised society, until we passed over an isolated building which from the air looked very much like the others, except that it was larger and there were three cars parked fairly near it. I pointed down and said: 'There'. We circled, saw a possible landing place about half a mile away and descended near a beach, where a party of men were packing up some land-sea rescue equipment with which they had been practising. They were speaking Irish, but answered the pilot's enquiry about coffee in English. The pilot, Peter Peckowski, speaks with a slight Polish accent. By all means they said, but doubtfully. Coffee is not very usual in remote Ireland. They led us over ditches and by tracks to the roadway and there, in front of us, was the building I had spotted from the air. It was a public house.

'Tell me', said one of the men, 'did youse ever drink tea?'

I assured him we had.

Inside the women of the house went off to make the coffee without fuss, while Peter asked where we were.

'In Ballydavid', said the owner, 'if you go by the map, but the right name is Baile na nGall'.

I was sitting at one of the tables and said: 'The town of the

Strangers'.

He hadn't expected that and came over to scrutinise me.

'You're not foreign', he said.

'I am not', I said.

'Irish'.

'That's so'.

He looked more closely.

'You have the look of a Dublin man?'

'Now you have it'.

'A writer maybe?'

'Correct'.

'James Plunkett?'

It was embarrassing. It was also, quite unexpectedly, deeply moving to be recognised in my own country so far away from my own small world.

'Pleased to meet you', I said.

If he had presented me with the Freedom of Dingle, I wouldn't have been so genuinely honoured and I felt, not for the first time, that before I die I will speak my native language adequately enough to talk with those of my countrymen who have it from birth, so that they won't shame me by having to change to English on my account.

3

Later, when we returned to Castletownbere, we circled what remains of Dunboy Castle. It stands on a promontory with the Atlantic spreading in front of it and at one time it belonged to a powerful Irish Prince, O'Sullivan Beare. He too, an ally of the Great O'Neill, was a victim of the defeat at Kinsale and his castle was bombarded to smithereens in a last stand which for heroism and hopelessness outclasses anything in romantic fiction. Following its destruction O'Sullivan managed to withdraw with the remnants of his clan to the fastnesses of Glengarriff. Here his fighting men guarded the passes against attack for six months, while deer-hunting and fishing supported the refugees. It worked until winter came, when O'Sullivan had four hundred fighting men left to guard six hundred non-combatants consisting of women and children, servants and the aged and infirm. On the last day of December 1602 he made his decision to fight his way north, a journey of two or three hundred miles, taking with him all his dependants, including the sick and the wounded. It meant literally hacking his way from Glengarriff to Leitrim through country which was entirely subdued and infested with English forces. Word was sent through the country by the Lord President calling on all 'on peril of being treated as O'Sullivan's covert or open abettors, to fall upon him, to cross his road, to bar his way, to watch for him at fords, to come upon him by night; and above all, to drive off or destroy all cattle or other possible means of sustenance, so that of sheer necessity his party must perish on the way. Whose lands soever O'Sullivan would be found to have passed through unresisted, or whereupon he was allowed to find food of any kind, the Government would consider forfeit.'

O'Sullivan travelled by the Pass of Keimaneigh to Agharis which lies between Gougane Barra and Macroom; then northwards between Charleville and Buttevant to the traditional refuge of the hunted and defeated, the vast solitude of the Glen of Aherlow, holding off skirmishes and guerrilla attacks and fighting pitched battles which were won against enormously superior forces by sheer desperation. He crossed Slieve Felim and at Portland they entrenched themselves while they prepared to cope with the great, natural barrier, the Shannon river. Eleven horses were slain, their hides used to make a boat and the flesh eaten and in that way, harassed still by their pursuers, they made the crossing. At Aughrim they fought a pitched battle against a force of eight hundred which barred their path and again, driven by desperation, burst their way through. They crossed Slieve Muire (Mount Mary) and pushed on by out-of-the-way paths and through deep snowdrifts. Eventually when they at last reached O'Rourke's castle at Dromahair in County Leitrim, the party consisted of eighteen non-combatants and only sixteen armed men. Within a few days about fifty more straggled in; the rest of the company of one thousand had either strayed, or succumbed to exposure and fatigue, or had been slain.

In 1603 Lord Deputy Mountjoy was writing to the Privy Council 'All that are out doe seeke for mercy excepting O'Rorke and O'Sullivan, who is now with O'Rorke'.

In 1604 O'Sullivan, despairing of effective resistance, sailed for Spain and the Court of King Philip where, having been received with honour and granted lodging and a pension, he was murdered in the suburbs of Madrid on his way from Mass.

The stump of Dunboy Castle still stands at the water's edge outside the town of Castletownbere, surrounded by a small wood in which herons nest. Beside it, in 1920, a Welsh-born landowner built an enormous mansion, Puxley Hall, which is in ruins also. When I asked about it locally at first I could get no information, until perseverance forced one man to talk.

'It got burned', he said. I knew he was being evasive and I also knew why. He thought I was British because I was with the BBC crew and felt the truth might be unnecessarily insulting to my country—after all, we were guests.

'Who burned it?' I asked.

'Damn the bit of me knows', he said.

'Was it the boys?' I asked.

He was basically an honest man.

After a struggle he gave in.

'Now that you mention it', he said, as though the recollection had just come to him, 'I believe it was'.

So Dunboy Castle and Puxley Hall stand in ruins together, the one razed to the ground by the army of Elizabeth, the other burned out by Irish rebels. Three hundred years and more separate them in time and yet they are very close to one another; not merely contiguous, but close in the sense Louis MacNeice meant when he wrote:

> . . . as close
> As the peasantry were to the landlord,
> As the Irish to the Anglo-Irish,
> As the killer is close one moment
> To the man he kills,
> Or as the moment itself
> Is close to the next moment.

6

No Tree Whereon to Hang a cMan

ON a bright March morning we left Shannon Airport to follow the estuary of the Shannon where it forms the western border of County Clare. For helicopter filming they take the door off, a procedure which for the first ten minutes or so leaves you fingering your safety belt and expecting (as the man said) every minute to be your next. After a while, however, the exhilaration of cruising above land and sea with the wind whipping about you takes over.

It was a journey above a sun-dazzled panorama of white sand flats, chilled blue water patterned by grey and green streams where the treacherous sea currents flowed through it, and bronze sea growths waving in the depths. The fields on either side, sheltering in their patchwork of stone walls, had not yet lost their lean winter look, which made it easier to see the outlines of the ring forts built for defence and daily living long before the beginnings of written history. They were so numerous that we gave up trying to count them, but it was obvious that the almost empty landscape below us had once teemed with human beings living closely in community along the banks of what must be Ireland's oldest highway.

Scattery Island, which can be reached by boat from Kilrush,

offered evidence of a later culture in the remains of its churches and its Round Tower. Its monastery was founded in the 6th century by St. Senan, who, like Kevin of Glendalough is also said to have been followed to his retreat by a woman—a holy woman this time who wished only to set up her hut near his saintly presence. Like Kevin he wasn't having any and chased her away.

Carrigaholt and its ruined castle where Charles O'Brien, who fought at Ramillies in 1706 and became a Marshal of France, once lived, brought history forward again by over a thousand years. The famous 'Clare's Dragoons' were trained there before the battle. Then came the sheer cliffs of Loop Head and the chasm which is known as Cuchulainn's Leap, because the hero jumped it to escape the advances of an amorous Hag who fell and was drowned when she tried to leap after him, a story from the mists of pre-history. It brought the reflection that Irish saints and heroes, pagan and Christian, seem to have had unending trouble with women. From Loop Head the views in good weather are magnificent; Dingle Peninsula to the south, the Aran Islands due north, and inland, beyond Galway city, the unmistakable purple shapes of the Connemara Mountains.

Clare has the Shannon looping it from east to south and the ocean providing its western boundary, barriers which give it a natural isolation. Its seaboard is the very edge of Europe and acts the part. From Loop Head northwards to Black Head, the sea beats at dark cliffs which seem always to be in silhouette, or rolls in across wide beaches which were once cluttered with the wreckage of the ships of the Spanish Armada. The cliffs of Moher rise seven hundred feet above the sea and extend for five miles, so sheer and inhospitable that even the sea birds seem to have despaired of finding any shelter for nesting. In misty weather they look even more enormous, like the nightmare of some deranged God; in fine weather, particularly at sunset, they belong still to mythology and the underworld. I remember one magnificent evening of calm sea and barely perceptible wind, when they seemed, for all their dark and massive brutality, to have become weightless in a world of such liquidity and colour that it was impossible to say if the ocean was reflecting the sky or the sky the ocean. Reds and yellows, silvers and greens were spilling and spreading above and below. At a little distance it seemed, the Aran Islands, darkly outlined, were rocking gently and ready to set sail. Above them and beyond them and all around them the universe was about to melt away in ecstasy. At that moment it was easy to understand the old tales of fabulous islands where age was stayed forever and happiness eternal. At one time such sunsets were the birth of gods and the beginning of sagas.

Inland lies the Burren country. It too, seems to belong to another age, or even another world. It is a plateau of bare lime-stone, miles and miles of fissured rock which looks like a lunar landscape. In the bad old days someone said of it: 'Not a tree whereon to hang a man; no water in which to drown him; no soil in which to bury him'.

Yet for all its bare and inhospitable appearance, the rocky crevices are rich in rare plants of arctic and Alpine and Mediter-ranean origin which delight the naturalist and turn its grey acres into a vast rock garden in springtime. A skin of soil gathered in a crevice provides nourishment and the rocky sides give shelter and protection. Even in primitive times man drove his cattle to the Burren for winter feeding.

The soft, wet Atlantic winds keep the sea forever present in the Burren country, so that its acres of grey rock breathe a salt smell that conjures up the dawn of creation. In the Beginning, surely, was the Burren.

John Betjeman wrote of it.

> Stony, seaboard, far and foreign,
> Stony hills poured over space,
> Stony outcrop of the Burren,
> Stones in every fertile place,
> Little fields with boulders dotted,
> Grey stone shoulders saffron spotted
> Stone-walled cabins thatched with reeds
> Where a Stone age people breeds
> The last of Europe's stone age race.

I mentioned earlier Saint Colman who had three pets: a cock,

a mouse and a fly. He built his hermitage in the Burren country on the slopes of Sliabh Corran. There is a story that at the end of Lent Colman and his servant had no food to break their long, penitential fast. Meanwhile a feast was taking place at the palace of Colman's half brother, King Guaire, which was at Kinvara in Co. Galway, some miles away. The saint, taking pity on his servant, caused the dishes to be lifted from under the noses of the King's guests and wafted over the hills to the hermitage. The guests, not unnaturally, wondered what was happening. They took horse and followed the dishes. In this way King Guaire found his half brother and was so pleased about it that he caused a monastery to be built for him, the present Kilmacduagh, which dates back to 610. The saint is buried to the west of it. The trail of the dishes is known locally as Bothar na Mios. Those with good eyesight and a little imagination can still see the marks of the horses' hooves and the brown stains left by the gravy that spilled over from the dishes. The remains of the hermitage are more difficult to find in the tangle of bushes and trees which have choked them. Dun Guaire keeps up the feasting tradition in a nightly banquet which is given for visitors during the holiday season. To the best of my knowledge, there has been no modern recurrence of the disappearing dishes incident.

Feakle, a village in the Slieve Aughty Mountains is the birthplace of Brian Merriman whose famous poem (in the Irish language) *The Midnight Court* was written somewhere around 1790, and has been translated by a number of writers into English, the most controversial version being Frank O'Connor's which was banned twice by the Censorship Board. They may have given up banning it since then, for I've seen O'Connor's version published since, but at the time it caused an uproar. When some opponents in an effort to clear the good name of Irish literature, suggested that the translation was entirely O'Connor's own work, Frank regretted it wasn't true, but remarked that it was the only compliment Ireland had ever paid

Lahinch. *The soft, wet Atlantic winds keep the sea forever present . . .*

Dun Guaire Castle. *Meanwhile a feast was taking place at the palace of Colman's half brother, King Guaire.*

him. When a fund was started to erect a memorial over Merriman's grave in Feakle, despite the fact that President de Valera was the first subscriber, the Clare County Council wouldn't allow it. When the money collected was spent on publishing a new edition of the translation, that too was banned. Honour-and-Virtue was again triumphant, the suggestion that there was any kind of red blood in the Irish heritage was as usual stamped out. Things have changed now, I am glad to say, and a Merriman Summer School is attended regularly by the most respectable people.

These are matters easily absorbed into the tranquillity of the Clare countryside, where the friaries and abbeys brood on the impermanence of even God's earthly residences and lonely castles seem to be keeping up some secret soliloquy with their past. Evils and angers pass away; virtue is no more permanent, though it sometimes leaves a breath of its having been: only resignation and acceptance persist, in the turn of a phrase, the set of the features, a tone in the voice or the inherited gesture of the hands.

2

Somewhere along the Clare coast I sat in a public house one morning and listened to an old lady telling me a story. She was almost eighty years of age, slim and straight in a black dress. She had grey hair and a light, girlish voice and eyes that relived all she was saying. Her sister, who may have been some years younger, acted as chorus, now and then nodding her head or confirming something with a couple of words or a smile when asked for corroboration. The doors were open to the sunlit street where nothing in particular was happening. You could hear the sea and even distinguish its smell among the faint impregnations of the pub.

I had mentioned the hotel I was staying in, a beautiful house in its own grounds, and wondered who had owned it originally. She said it had once been the Big House of the area, owned by an arrogant landlord (whom she named).

'When I was a small child', she said, 'they had great gates there and they kept them closed. No one of the locals was allowed in, unless it was a tradesman or someone on business, or the children taking a short cut to school. Whenever we wished to do that we had to keep at a certain distance from the house and then, when we were leaving by the far gate, we had to open our bags or our baskets or whatever we were carrying our few books in, to be examined in case we had taken anything off the ground or had plucked any of the flowers. There were wild flowers in the woods, but you were not allowed to touch those either, not even for the May Altar that we used to make in the classroom

(Overleaf) . . . *a tiny light into the labyrinthine tenacity of the Irish soul.*

during that month of the year. They were Protestants like the rest of the landowners, and as bitter as you'd care to meet.'

'At one time the Christian Brothers came to the village to set up a school. Someone gave them a piece of wasteland as a playground for the children. It was a small piece of ground and no use to anyone else but it was up to the wall of the estate and the landlord didn't relish it. It was the Christian Brothers he didn't like, of course, not the little children. First he complained of the noise the children made when they were playing, though they were so far away from the house, with a high wall between them and all the length of the grounds between, that he'd want a powerful pair of ears to hear them. But when the Brothers seemed to pay no attention to his complaints, he got the servants to dump all the rubbish they could find over the wall. They did so every day, anything that came to hand, as well as the waste food from the kitchen and the bits and scraps you would keep for pigs and hens; all that kind of rubbish and waste and even (you'll know what I'm referring to now) even worse than that. So in the end the playground was in no fit state for any child to play in and the Brothers had to leave it to him. I remember that well and I remember my own mother saying what a shame it was. But it was the Big House, so what could anyone do.

'But you see there can be no luck in a bigot or a begrudger and that one was no different from the rest. In the troubled times, when the boys were burning out the landlords, good, bad or indifferent, he began to change his tune. There was this young fellow, a tradesman that was regularly up and down to the Big House, and he was well known as an officer in the I.R.A. He was there so often that we all knew, and the landlord knew, that it wasn't business that was bringing him at all; it was one of the daughters had taken a fancy to him, and him to her. The landlord said nothing because it was all a different story now and he was afraid to. Until one day the two of them went off together and got married. There was murder that time. He cut her off from her inheritance, he closed his gates against the rest of the world, he took every revenge he could on the business of the local people.

'The rest of us waited to see what would happen and it wasn't long until it came about. I suppose they would have burned him out like they did many another except for the daughter being the wife of who she was. So they paid him a visit in the usual style one night, with petrol cans and revolvers. They gave him a time limit: leave the house with what he could carry with him or have it burned down about his ears.

'In those times there was little the police or anybody else could do; they had enough on their minds trying to keep their barracks from going up in smoke—and the landlord knew it. He said he'd think it over. "You can think it over until the day after to-morrow (that was a Thursday)", they told him, "and if you're not gone altogether from the village by twelve o'clock in the middle of that day we'll do what we should be doing now if we'd any sense at all".

'On the Thursday we all waited. There were no police about and nothing unusual of any kind, except that there was no business being done and hardly anyone abroad. Then, sometime before the hour, the gates opened and the landlord rode out in a horse and trap with one of his servants at the reins. They drove down the street that was empty and they drove out the road there towards the bridge. I was watching them with my sister here. They crossed the bridge and went out of sight on the other side and at that moment, the Angelus bell began to strike and it was twelve o'clock.'

Her sister said it was all true, she remembered it well.

'What happened to him after that I don't know', the old lady continued. 'He went abroad I suppose, or whatever, but he must surely be dead by now. But I saw something else that I won't forget, something I thought often enough about since. There was an auction of the house afterwards and then an auction of the furniture and all the bits and pieces. The local people were there, some of them to buy, some of them to gape, for they'd never been inside such a house in their lives. There were farmers from around the neighbourhood too. One of these bought a few things, and with them a couple of fine beds. He had an ass and cart with him and when he loaded the beds on to it he had nothing to tie them down with. He asked me if I knew where there might be a piece of rope or some such thing, but I didn't and was too young and shy to help him even if I did. By that time the auctioneer had gone, the house was empty only for a few men that were tidying up. The farmer walked back again into the house with myself following and he looked here and he looked there. Then his eye fell on a bell pull which was set beside a great, marble fireplace. It was a long silk rope, woven together with red and yellow threads, which you pulled on to summon the servants when you had need. The farmer looked at this for a while, then he reached up his hand and gave a couple of powerful tugs. The bell made a terrible jangling right through the house as though it would jump from its socket and the rope was torn from its place on the wall. Then I saw the farmer taking the rope outside with him and tying it about the beds on his ass and cart to make them secure. He went off down the drive with the beds and the bits and pieces and the silk rope—it was the most beautiful silk rope you had ever seen—and the place was empty. I thought to myself: there goes the way of all pride. And I thought to myself again: there will be nobody now to search the baskets or humiliate a little child, and they may pick the wild flowers to their hearts' content.'

That was the story the old lady told me. She was, as I said, near to eighty. Yet the shame and resentment of childhood was still fresh in her mind. I thought of another man, a labourer for a Meath landlord, whose punishment for some piece of negligence was to be made to stand at attention outside the study window of his master for the whole of the livelong day, in sight of his workmates and, a worse humiliation, his own wife and children. It is not hard to imagine what seeds of hatred and vengeance may have taken root in those long hours of silence, immobility and shame.

In the evening I took the road north from the Burren into South Galway, where bare rock gives way to bogland and woodland and the city itself, understanding well the terrible wrath of those who are wronged and dispossessed, placed a curious inscription over its West Gate:

From the fury of the O'Flahertys,
good Lord deliver us.

7

The Prince and the Merlins

THERE is a story by Liam O'Flaherty called 'Going Into
Exile' in which the son and daughter of an Aran household
are dressed for the first time in their lives in shop-bought
clothes. It is the last night they will spend on the island before
leaving to seek their livelihood in the United States and the
neighbours are gathered in the kitchen to wish them God speed.
All night the windows of the cottage are ablaze, all night the
sounds of music and dancing fill the little fields in their maze of
stone walls and the narrow roadways that are strewn with
patches of blown sand. In the morning, when the American
Wake is over and the time has come to leave forever, the young
man picks a flake of loose whitewash from the wall of his island
home and puts it carefully in his pocket. Then he and his sister
set off down the roadway towards the island harbour and the
sound of the sea. It is a story that returned to my mind the first
time I set foot on the islands and, remembering it afresh, I
wondered how many young men from the cottages about me,
who are now assimilated into the urban life and routines of
crowded cities, had sought in their time to keep captive in a
flake of lime or a pebble from the shore the wide skies of home
and the vast panorama of the sea.

The Aran Islands lie about thirty miles off the Galway coast.
At the turn of the century, for the founders of the Irish Literary
Revival and for scholars searching for Gaelic Ireland's eclipsed

language and life, they were a place of pilgrimage. W. B. Yeats and his brother Jack, Lady Gregory and Arthur Symons, paid their homage in turn. J. M. Synge, abandoning Paris and the study of French literature, found in the life of the islands the fugitive reality he had searched County Wicklow for and, in addition, the basic material for at least four of his plays. There are three islands: Inishmore, the largest, where Liam O'Flaherty was born; Inishmaan, the middle island; and Inisheer, the smallest and most easterly. Apart from the occasional scholar, to-day's visitors are mainly students and schoolchildren, who go there to study Irish in one of the few places left where it is still the everyday language.

I made the journey myself on a morning when the waters in the bay were in one of their blacker moods. The Naomh Eanna, which is a bit punch-drunk even at the best of times, staggered its way through whipping winds and giant, spray-scattering waves. She was packed tight with schoolchildren, all of them stuffed unwisely with lemonade and crisps and most of them regretting it. The choice was to stay below and get sick or stay on deck and get soaked. I settled for being wet. Up above us the BBC helicopter was filming our misery. For once the fact aroused hardly any interest. The priority was to keep body and soul together.

We were to land first at Inisheer but weather conditions prevented it, so we made for Inishmaan instead and stood-to about a quarter of a mile off land, where there was enough shelter to relax after the battering and wait to be taken ashore.

At first nothing seemed likely to happen at all. We were not expected, and across the intervening stretch of sea the curve of the strand gleamed white and empty and the small fields beyond were deserted, as though everybody was late at breakfast. The first sign of life was a small dog, a black blob on the wide strand which began to race towards the water's edge. It was followed by a man. In seconds a few more men appeared, all hurrying. Then suddenly there was activity everywhere. Men with upturned currachs on their shoulders began to converge on the beach from all corners, surrounded by racing children and scores of dogs. The women were gathering too, but more

Carrying a Currach. *Men with upturned currachs on their shoulders began to converge on the beach.*

demurely. Soon the currachs were spread out over the sea, a fleet of bobbing shells that disappeared and re-appeared among the waves, all rowing steadily for the ship. These bobbing corks with their flimsy canvas covering would be our transport to dry land when we reached Inisheer, so we studied them with more than academic interest as the men of Inishmaan unloaded post and provisions for the island. Later, at Inisheer, the scene repeated itself, except that this time the pier was already crowded and the people ready to receive us. We made the trip to the shore in the island's fleet of currachs and the children scattered to the island homes where they were to spend their holiday living as members of the family.

It was, as I have said, my first visit to the islands and the first thing I saw was a group of people kneeling on the shore to receive the blessing of a newly ordained priest, believed to be highly efficacious. The first person I met was a young writer who had thrown up his job with some local authority on the mainland and retired to Inisheer to finish the novel he was working on. By a very sensible and simple reversal of the usual, he was living on the pension contributions that had been returned to him. The second person I met was the publican, which was only right. The third was a sergeant of police, whose duties in the matter of crime are practically non-existent. The Church Visible was represented by Father Gilligan, who lives on Inisheer and ministers both there and on Inishmaan, each household taking it in turn to transport him from one island to the other. As I talked with him on the beach he held up his open fingers against the western horizon and invited me to look through them. They were black shadows against the sun.

'Those things sticking up in front of you', he said, 'are the chimney stacks of New York'.

And again Liam O'Flaherty's story came to mind. New York has more reality for the Aran Islander and is less remote than Dublin, because for generations the emigration drift has been to America. Remittances from sons and daughters who have settled in the United States are an accepted part of island economy.

Limestone rock covers the islands in great fissured slabs, similar to the Burren area in Clare, but generations of islanders have toiled to make small fields by blocking the crevices with stones and spreading alternate layers of sand and seaweed to manufacture soil for their potatoes. They have raised stone walls to protect the growing crops and made rough stone troughs to collect and store rainwater for cattle and for irrigation. The result is a maze of tiny fields and narrow roadways which slope down eastwards to great beaches of fine, white sand, broken here and there by clusters of upturned currachs. Fishing is one of the mainstays of life and the currach, which the islander learns to handle almost from infancy, is both a symbol of the islands and an essential part of their economy. The sea is at once benefactor and enemy; it supports life—it also kills. When Synge wrote *Riders To The Sea* he was dealing not only with a poetic truth but with the tragic reality. The sons of many an island family have been claimed by the sea. Storms have drowned their share, but the deadliest killer of all is fog, which can descend suddenly and last for days, so that the boatmen lose their sense of direction and drift around at the mercy of thirst and exposure.

All three islands have their antiquities. Dun Aonghusa on Inishmore is one of the finest pre-historic forts in Western Europe, with a triple rampart and outer defences, the first of which consists of a fifty foot barrier of large stones set upright in the ground. Early Christian remains date back to the 6th century when monasticism was introduced by St. Enda. One of them, on Inisheer, is the ruined church of St. Cavan, who is supposed to have been a brother of Kevin of Glendalough. It stands on the summit of a sandhill overlooking the beach, and every year the winter storms bury its ruins and the graves about it in drifting sand. But they are not lost or forgotten. I have a feeling that on Aran nothing worthwhile ever is. On the saint's feast day in June of each year, the islanders clear away the mountain of sand, candles are lit once again in the shell of the Church and the people pray there. There are the usual stories of cures, but that is not the point. The point is that the mass bell has rung out over the islands for well over a thousand years: once for monks and unlettered people, now for schoolchildren from the cities, for scholars and for the local people from whom they learn. Aran, cut off from the mainland by those thirty miles of ocean and clinging to traditional skills and a simple economy, has held about itself (and is, one feels, conscious still of holding about itself) the remnants of a civilisation that, after the fall of Hugh O'Neill, Earl of Tyrone, was crushed out of existence almost everywhere else in Ireland. An ancient world, long departed, has left its discarded image in that mirror.

2

When Henry VIII assumed the title of King of Ireland in 1541 English influence, although they had been here already for four centuries, hardly extended outside Dublin and the bigger

St. Cavan's Church, Inisheer. *On the Saint's feast day in June of each year, the islanders clear away the mountain of sand, candles are lit once again and the people pray there.*

towns. Beyond these, and especially in the northern portion of Ireland, the old Gaelic way of life continued, largely unaffected by English law. It was quite a different civilisation, different in language and its sense of values, in its law and social structures. It was ancient, admirable, and archaic.

The Irish by nature and preference were country dwellers. Their wealth was in crops and huge herds of cattle; their houses were built of timber or wattle in the ancient way; their strongholds for the most part were crannogs (artificial lake islands) or raths. An occasional stone fort acknowledged the progress of techniques and thinking in the world beyond them; otherwise they were content to speak their own language and cultivate a way of life distinctive in its music, its poetry, its sagas, its pride in blood and genealogy. If wars disturbed them frequently it was in the usual pattern of cattle raids or the feuding and rivalries of their Chiefs. Although there had been attempts from time to time by the more powerful kings to impose some form of centralised authority they had failed to effect any permanent change. Gaelic Ireland remained a country of autonomous statelets with shifting allegiances, living, as it were, on the tributes they extracted from each other as fortune waxed or waned. You have only to look at the old maps. Topographically they may be largely fictional; politically they reveal a perilous situation, in which small territories, labelled 'The countrie of O'Boyle', 'The countrie of MacSorley', 'Harry Oge's countrie', 'The Countrie of O'Kane' and a hundred others all elbow each other with individualistic arrogance and self-absorption. Although the Irish Way of Living had some meaning, however undefined, for the O'Kanes and the Harry Oges, the larger concept of Ireland as a nation seems to have been quite beyond them.

England, on the other hand, had progressed to a concept of centralised authority which in Elizabeth's reign produced a material power for which the Englishman has been much hated ever since, and a burst of cultural activity which cannot be too highly regarded, not only in her dramatists and poets but in her musicians who, although burdened with such unfortunate names as Dr. Bull and Dr. Blow, were nevertheless the great Contrapuntists. There could be no doubt of the outcome for Ireland, it seemed, when England determined on the big push to conquer her.

Yet when it came, near the close of the 16th century, it very nearly misfired altogether, precisely because it encountered in the person of Hugh O'Neill, Earl of Tyrone, the one Irish leader educated by England itself to understand the strength of England's political organisation and the weakness of the Irish.

It had been English policy to acknowledge individual chiefs from among rival claimants by accepting token submission from them, giving them the title of Earl, and then confirming their overlordship in the territories they controlled, on condition that they accepted English law. Many of them made their submission, which appeared to be nominal, only to find that their territories had now been opened to the legitimate incursions of English Judges and officials and to the erection of English strongpoints. In Hugh O'Neill Elizabeth went a step further. He was the likely successor to the powerful chieftainship of Tyrone, a substantial and completely unsubjugated northern territory. Elizabeth brought him to England as a child to be educated there. An English upbringing, it was thought, followed by the prospect of an English title which would secure him in his right to his Irish territory, might induce him to suffer the same introduction of English law and practice among his people. Some time after Hugh had returned to Ireland he was, on Elizabeth's agreement, made Earl of Tyrone. For a while the plan worked, in so far as he fought side by side with his English patrons, in their war against the rebellious Earl of Desmond. His loyalty seemed to be sincere and he was given an allowance to help him guard the peace in Ulster, with permission to keep six companies of soldiers for the same purpose.

Being recognised by the Crown as Earl of Tyrone meant security, at least for a time, but the inherent disadvantages began to irk O'Neill. As Earl of Tyrone he was, like the rest, committed to the English system. As Irish Chief of his clan, under the Irish system, he would have absolute authority and the unfettered inheritance due to his Blood. The influence of life among the Tyrone clansmen, his close connection with other Ulster Chiefs who were at loggerheads with the Government, and his first-hand knowledge of the impermanence of English promises eroded his belief in his personal position. Again, with the increasing pressures to push the Protestant Reformation, religious loyalty became an active issue and Ireland generally began to look to Spain and France as possible sources of help. O'Neill showed his sympathies very clearly in this regard when he succoured some of the survivors of the Spanish Armada and got them safely away to Scotland, a treasonable act punishable

(Opposite) Illustration to an Elizabethan map of Ireland.

The Gentleman of Ireland   The Gentlewoman of Ireland

The Wild: Irish man   The Wilde Irish Woman

by death. He saw his brother-in-law, Red Hugh O'Donnell, heir to the chieftainship of Tyrconnell, seized by a trick and imprisoned in Dublin Castle. To complicate matters further, he fell in love with Mabel Bagenal, who eloped with him. It was a grave matter. Her brother, who was Elizabeth's Chief Marshal of Ireland at the time, was infuriated and swore vengeance. O'Neill eventually abandoned all pretence to loyalty. He had himself inaugurated as The O'Neill on the hill of Tullaghogue, reverting to the ancient Gaelic manner of his clan, an act which symbolised his utter rejection of the English system. He was in open rebellion.

Soon there was an army in the field against him. He was not unprepared. The law had allowed him six companies of soldiers. It had not said they must always be the same soldiers, so he had changed them completely whenever they were properly trained. He had imported quantities of lead under licence for the roofs of his houses. He had made firm alliances with other chiefs so that, with the encouragement of his initial success in a number of impressive victories, his rebellion became a national uprising. Philip II of Spain was sued for help and a strong confederacy of Ulster Chiefs prepared for total war under Hugh O'Neill's leadership, finding in him:

'at last, a man of real greatness, a statesman as well as a soldier, a born leader who combined thought with action and caution with energy, no out-of-date Gaelic Chief intent on his own rights and wrongs, but a man of intellect who understood his times and who called on Ireland to combine all her wrongs and seek redress as a united nation. The great rising began in the North with an alliance of Tyrconnell and Tyrone, formerly hostile, and while the elder Hugh proved to be a cautious leader, in Red Hugh O'Donnell was found a lieutenant, a young hero, and the forward fighter of the cause' (E. Curtis: *A History of Ireland*).

For five years a state of rebellion existed. O'Neill won his battles, but fought them only when he had to. He had no siege equipment and no field guns with which to attack the big towns. His hopes and those of his allies, were centred on the promises of men and equipment from Spain. Only if the ships of Philip were on the high seas could he hope for permanent victory over his enemies. The watchers searched the seas about Ireland, waiting anxiously for the fulfilment of a promise while O'Neill fought to hold the upper hand. They sought in vain. As the years passed English military strength built up and opportunity trickled away. When Spanish help came at last under Don Juan del Aguilla, they landed at Kinsale in the extreme South, quite inexplicably, since it left the whole length of Ireland between them and the army they were supposed to assist. They were immediately surrounded and besieged, so that instead of helping O'Neill, he was forced to march from the extreme north to the extreme south in an effort to relieve them. The operation was beyond his resources. He was defeated, his army broken and his northern stronghold rendered defenceless.

The English forces, seizing the opportunity, burst into Tyrone, coming down from Derry and over from Antrim and up from Armagh by causeways and forest paths and the hidden ways that had been denied to them for so long. The cattle were driven off, the cornfields trampled and burned. The Queen's viceroy ran up St. George's Cross above O'Neill's ruined castle of Dungannon. To emphasise the full meaning of his victory he ordered his men to climb the hill of Tullaghogue to shatter the stone chair which for centuries had been the inaugural seat of The O'Neills. The hammer strokes at Tullaghogue on that September day of 1602 sounded the knell not of O'Neill's sovereignty alone, but of the old Gaelic civilisation and order.

As the English continued to strengthen their advantage, Hugh's personal danger increased. At last, in 1607, while he was at Slane Castle on the river Boyne, word was brought that a French ship had arrived in Lough Swilly to take himself and the Earl of Tyrconnell to Spain. O'Neill regarded it as an opportunity to make a direct appeal to the King of Spain for military assistance. Although armed help never materialised, a sketch of his journey and his ultimate fate may, I think, be of interest. He went first to the house of his old friend and ally Sir Garret More at Mellifont to take his farewell, 'weeping abundantly at his departure' (say the chroniclers) 'and giving a solemn farewell to every child and every servant in the house, which made them marvel, because in general it was not his manner to use such compliments'.

He rode north, staying for two days at his old residence in Dungannon. Then, travelling all night, he hurried on to Rathmullen on Lough Swilly where in company with more than eighty others he set off for Spain. So, on 14th day of September 1607, the feast of the Holy Cross, began the Flight of The Earls, an event recorded and deplored in the Annals of the Four Masters: 'Woe to the heart that meditated, woe to the mind that conceived, woe to the council that decided on the project of their setting out on this voyage . . . Tonight Ireland is desolate. The banishment of her true race hath left wet-cheeked her men and her fair women—strange that such a dwellingplace should be so desolate'.

Tadhg Ó Cianáin, who was scribe to the Maguires, and who took ship with the Earls, recorded their journey and their adventures in a chronicle which is at present in the keeping of the Franciscan Order at Killiney (Co. Dublin). The journal, which is in Irish, describes their departure:

> 'Then they proceeded out to sea to make for Spain straight-forward if they could. After that they were on the sea for thirteen days with excessive storm and dangerous bad weather. A cross of gold which O'Neill had, and which contained a portion of the Cross of the Crucifixion and many other relics, being put by them in the sea trailing after the ship, gave them great relief'.

Even in 1607, it will be seen, we are still very near to the belief of the early Gaelic monks in miracles and Angelic intervention.

Ó Cianáin goes on:

> 'At the end of that time, much to their surprise, they met in the middle of the sea two small hawks, merlins, which alighted on the ship. The hawks were caught and fed afterwards. About midnight the sea rose in violent, quick, strong-sounding waves against them. It was the mercy of the Trinity

that saved them and kept the ship and all that were in it from being drowned.'

After twenty-one days at sea O'Neill and his retinue landed safely at a little town on the river Seine called Quilleboeuf, where they were entertained lavishly by the Governor and in return, as a token of their gratitude, they presented to him the two little hawks they had saved from the sea, a detail which for some reason reads very movingly in the journal. Bad weather made it impossible for them to sail directly to Spain, so O'Neill looked for permission to make the journey through France. The English Ambassador demanded that the King of France should refuse them, which for diplomatic reasons he did; but he allowed them free passage to Flanders. The Ambassador objected to this too, but was snubbed.

At Louvain again the English persuaded the Spanish Ambassador to withhold travelling permission, so O'Neill thought to go by way of Lorraine, Switzerland and Italy. Immediately the Duke of Lorraine was warned that 'His Majesty King James the First of England will be greatly displeased if favourable entertainment is afforded to these fugitives'.

Meanwhile the spies dogged him and kept the Court informed of his every movement:

'O'Neill hath been at the Court of Beins, where it is said he was very favourably used by the Archduke, and was allowed the grace of personages of the greatest rank to speak with the Archduke *covered*'.

'Tyrone was again in this town two days since and lay a night at his son's lodging in Bruxelles'.

'The Earl of Tyrone, his wife and forty men of their crew arrived, by the way of Switzerland, this last week in Milan, on horseback, well armed with arquebusses and pistols, to the no small wonder of the beholders; the Governor here having formerly denied entrance into the city to persons with arms of that quality, even to the Ambassadors of great princes. But the Governor also, besides this favour, sent to them, immediately upon their arrival, his "cameriere maggiore", with banqueting stuff and such other refreshments, and with words of much affection'.

Despite the spies and the plots to hinder them, they entered Rome in state by the Piazza del Popolo and were received by the Pope on 5th May 1608 (O Cianáin reports) 'with kindness, with honour and with welcome'. Later on he records their attendance at Mass in St. Peter's:

> 'On Thursday 29th day of May 1608, Cardinal Borghese sent one of his noblemen as a grand messenger to invite the lords to solemn Mass which in honour of the Holy Father was celebrated in the great Church of St. Peter. A position of honour and a fitting place was selected for them close to and near the Pope'.

The spies were on to that too. We find James Roth, an agent who had insinuated himself into O'Neill's household service, writing to another agent in England. By arrangement with Lord Salisbury he adopted the guise of a Catholic writing to a fellow Catholic in England, which accounts for the pious and rather overdone reference to the holy picture and the Agnus Deis at the end.

> 'The Pope himself sang Mass. Overnight his holiness gave order that the Earl of Tyrone, and the rest with him, should have the best place in Church. I saw this order carried out. And to grace the matter more, his Holiness's niece went in coach to the Earl's house and brought with her to St. Peter's the Countess, giving her both in place and Church the better hand, which she also had of the Pope's sisters, amongst all the duchesses and other nobility of Rome.
>
> I send a picture of the newly canonized saint and forty Agnus Deis *and would send more if I had them*'.

But as the years dragged on neither argument, nor appeal, nor his pilgrimage to the seven privileged altars of St. Peter's, nor the power of his piece of the True Cross which once stilled the troubled waters about his ship, could persuade either the Pope or the King of Spain to equip him with arms and men to regain

The Pope receives the Great O'Neill. *Despite the spies and plots to hinder them they entered Rome in state by the Piazza del Popolo and were received by the Pope on 5th May, 1608.*

Ireland from his enemies. Gaelic Ireland was broken and doomed. With O'Neill in exile, the spoils could be seized and the proclamations began to fly.

'Whereas great scopes and extents of land in the several counties of Armagh, Tyrone, Coleraine, Donegal, Fermanagh and Cavan are escheated and come to our hands by the attainder of sundry traitors and rebels, we considered how much it would advance the welfare of that kingdom if the said land were planted with colonies of civil men and well-effected in religion; whereupon there was a project conceived for the division of the said lands into proportions, and for the distribution of the same unto undertakers . . .'

That was the beginning of the Plantation of Ulster, which laid the ground for Ireland's present division and the bitterness which is rending the North of Ireland to-day.

While his territories and those of his fellow earls were being distributed to those goodly men who were well effected in religion, O'Neill died in Rome and was buried at the Church of

149

Hibernus Miles. Illustration to an Elizabethan map of Ireland.

San Pietro in Montorio on 20th July 1616. He never got to Spain, nor did he return to Ireland. Surrounded at all times by spies and informers, his country divided among his enemies and her religion and language outlawed, he continued to petition for help. Though blindness afflicted him and age added to his difficulties, and though neither the Vatican nor Spain could supply him with the men and arms he sought for so persistently, we know, on the evidence of an agent's letter preserved among the State papers, that he clung desperately to hope. The spy wrote that sometimes in the evening after dining, if the aged Prince were warm with wine, his face would glow and he would strike the table and he would say:

Beidh lá geal gréine go fóill in Éirinn.
There will be a good day yet in Ireland.

There would, indeed. But it was to take another three hundred years.

8

A Memory of Dolphins

THE last time I drove towards Galway city a mist hung so low over everything that the countryside seemed to be slipping inch by inch under the sea. The long, grey stone walls gleamed with a skin of wet, the lichens oozed like sponges, the overhanging branches dripped great blobs of water. Grey skies and grey countryside measured each other pace by pace and mile by mile. Houses, when they dared to show themselves, looked huddled and uninhabited. The hens had disappeared from the farmyards, the birds had no heart to sing. A solitary bullock, half smothered in the fog of his own breath, gazed at nothing over a hedge and waited patiently for the end of the world. A day, you would think, when the damp must seep into the head, to be dozed away in some hotel bedroom or pushed to its dismal end with whiskey.

But no. Half an hour from the city a breeze began to blow holes in the mist here and there which spread out to join each other until they became patches of watery blue. The blue gradually deepened, the sun burst through. In a while the roads were steaming but clear and the landscape danced in the light.

Eyre Square was sunlit under a blue sky. An army band was playing there. And, as is usual with open air performances, it was turning a very ordinary afternoon into a festival. Young and old were standing around to listen, the dogs had gathered as they always do, people were smiling at each other to share the

151

general enjoyment in a way that never happens at concerts indoors. One countryman, who was obviously hard of hearing, had pulled his chair right up against the platform and cupped his ear while the brass blew great salvoes above him. The countrywomen sat surrounded by their enormous shopping bags, the countrymen had pushed their hats back on their heads and leaned forward on their sticks. At the end of each selection the conductor took a bow, the crowd applauded and cheered, the bandsmen grinned and shook the spit out of their instruments. For an hour or two live music performed under a sunny sky created that unique mood of innocence which is its special gift.

Galway gave the expression Lynch Law to the English language. Time has completely reversed its original meaning, but the incident that gave rise to it is still remembered. When James Lynch Fitzstephen was elected Mayor and Chief Magistrate of Galway in 1493, he was anxious to advance the welfare of the city by encouraging trade and good relations with Spain. On one of his trips to Cadiz he became friendly with an influential merchant called Gomez, whose son he took back with him to Galway as his guest. At first everything worked well and the Spanish merchant was delighted. Young Gomez and the magistrate's son Walter were of an age and became close friends. Influential townspeople were extremely hospitable. One of them, the father of Walter's girl friend Agnes, was also a merchant who spoke Spanish fluently, so young Gomez took great pleasure in visiting his house for conversation. After a while Walter became convinced that the centre of interest was not the father but Agnes herself. In a fit of jealous argument he lost control and in his fury stabbed young Gomez to death.

He fled to a hiding place near the town but within twenty-four hours an armed body of citizens, led by his own father, hunted him out. He was lodged in the gaol to await his trial, which would be conducted before his father, as Chief Magistrate. He was clearly guilty of the murder of a boy who was not only his close friend, but a guest of the city. The next day his father pronounced sentence of death in accordance with the law.

There was immediate reaction from his wife, who, as any

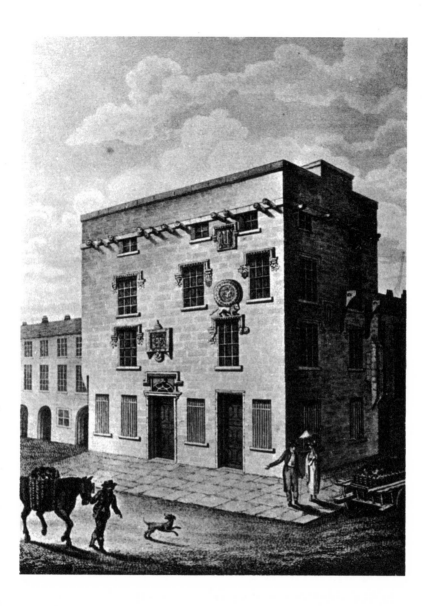

Lynch's Castle. *Lynch walked back to his house alone and unimpeded and the story is that he was never to set foot outside it afterwards.*

mother would, tried by entreaty and threats to have the sentence commuted. When these failed she roused her kinsfolk. On the morning of the execution father and son received the sacrament at the prison together and then proceeded to the place of execution. There was a confrontation between the escort and the factionists and feeling ran so high that when the execution spot was reached, there was no one with courage enough to carry out the law. Lynch stood up himself to face the threatening mob. After some minutes of tension and waiting, in which the duties of magistrate and father must have torn him apart, he stepped forward and carried out the act of execution himself.

The onlookers were dumbfounded at the deed, the threatening mob stupefied. Lynch walked back to his house alone and unimpeded and the story is that he was never seen to set foot outside it afterwards. The execution spot is at the site of the old gaol, near the Church of St. Nicholas in Lombard Street, where to-day an inscription on a black marble slab, surmounted by a death's head and crossbones, commemorates the incident.

'This memorial of the stern and unbending justice of the chief magistrate of this city, James Lynch Fitzstephen, elected Mayor A.D. 1493, who condemned and executed his own guilty son, Walter on this spot'

It was erected in 1624.

2

When I think of Galway city two pictures come automatically to mind. One is Albert Power's statue of the Gaelic writer Padraig O Conaire in Eyre Square, a diminutive figure with an abstracted air, his head bent as though he were listening to the band. Padraig wrote in a style which made concessions to modern concepts of form, a thing which was not approved at all by the more ardent language enthusiasts, certainly not any one of my own teachers, who set us a question on our favourite writer in Irish. When I wrote in honesty that mine was Padraig O Conaire (I think he was the only one I could read and understand) I was told to find another quick, because Padraig was anglicised.

Padraig O Conaire . . . *his head bent as though he were listening to the band.*

The other picture is Galway in race week some years ago, with the gaily painted caravans of the tinkers everywhere, followed by their strings of ponies and tribes of goats, the pedlars, the fruit sellers, the tipsters, the thimble riggers and the three card trick men. When I was young there was a three card trick man who operated every Sunday morning (weather, as they say, permitting) on the north quays of Dublin, opposite the Ha'penny Bridge. I got to know his line of guff practically by heart, so if I say that the three card trick men operating at Galway races were deplorable amateurs, I can claim to know what I am talking about.

The great weakness of the three card trick profession is that it has become surrounded by ritual. First there is the three card trick man himself, whose sleight of hand, coupled to his superior intellectual equipment, marks him off at once as the leader. He is entrusted with the properties; a small, collapsible table (designed to fold into invisibility at the approach of the Law), three cards of which one is a picture card and, of course, the money.

Next come his touts, already provided with money by the three card trick man himself, whose business it is, by their apparent success as gamblers, to arouse cupidity in the onlookers and persuade them to plunge.

When the crowd has gathered and all is ready the three card trick man manipulates the cards, showing the picture card (The Lady) and the others, and shuffling them around. Then he leaves them face downwards on the table and invites his audience to 'find the Lady'. If nobody ventures, tout No. 1 takes his cue. He behaves nervously, wets his lips, hesitates, then plunges ten shillings to a pound on one of the cards. He wins. The three card trick man reshuffles. Emboldened by his success, the tout selects a card again, has a pound to two pounds on it this time, and wins again. This double success is calculated to send up the emotional temperature of the onlookers. The three card trick man remains unmoved. He is happy to lose, he announces to everybody but, (with engaging frankness) happier still to win.

Tout No. 2 now comes forward, a pound clutched in his

hand. Tout No. 1 advises him to back the middle card, but the three card trick man notices this and re-shuffles the cards. Tout No. 1 pretends disgust. At this point however, the three card trick man, upset by the crush or uneasy about the police, turns his back on the table altogether. Seizing a glorious opportunity Tout No. 1 sneaks a look at the cards, which are face downwards, picks the lady and bends up one corner, so that however it may be re-shuffled, it will still be recognisable. With elaborate pantomime he conveys his cute dodge to Tout No. 2 who, when the cards are shuffled again, has no difficulty in selecting the one with the bent corner. He wins.

At this point the first Lamb is fixed on for encouragement by Tout No. 1. The corner of the card is still bent, the Tout points out in dumb show, the bet is a certainty. So the cards are shuffled and the Lamb plunges for a pound on the card with the bent corner. It is turned up. By some cruel mischance, possibly through a collision with the three card trick man's thumb during the shuffling, the corner of the picture card is straight again and one of the plain ones has become bent. The Lamb has seen the last of his pound. The Tout looks disgusted, the three card trick man is happy to lose, but happier still to win.

It is a time worn formula, interwoven with variations so unsubtle that the wonder is there are still people who are ignorant of it. At Galway races, instead of changing touts as he changed his pitch, the three card man kept the same two all the time, apparently oblivious of the fact that people at race meetings, including the potential lambs, are not planted firmly in the same piece of soil like a tree, but wander at will and are likely to remark the singularity of two people so dedicated to the person of the three card trick man that they stick to him like glue. To raise suspicion further, there was another remarkable factor. The three card trick man in question had fair hair and wore a blue suit with a brown shirt and a red tie. The tout who did most of the business of encouraging the Lambs by turning up the corner of the picture card when the three card trick man's attention was distracted had fair hair too. There was a remarkable family resemblance. Instead of trying to disguise it, however, he went out of his way to acknowledge it. He, too, wore a blue suit,

a brown shirt and a red tie. It underlines the need for an association of some sort, to enforce standards of competence. Otherwise the profession will get a bad name.

Galway, wedged between the sea and the great stretch of Lough Corrib, is the gateway to Connemara. In season, from the Weir Bridge spanning the Corrib river, hundreds of salmon can be seen lying on the bed of the river, waiting for the rain which will raise the levels so that they can pass up to their spawning grounds in the rivers and lakes which cover that scenically beautiful stretch of country. It begins properly when you cross the bridge beyond the village of Oughterard on the long and lovely journey to Clifden. Bogland with pools to reflect the sky, clumps of heather, lakes, brown streams, and blue mountains fill mile after mile. In a public house at Maam Cross I first heard Irish spoken as the everyday language by Herds who had been attending to their small Connemara sheep. At Cleggan, where you can buy your fish at the quayside straight from the boats, the best fish I have ever tasted, I saw the dolphins coming into the bay to play all day within a few yards of the shore. I remarked their scatterbrained antics to a fisherman and thought they were amusing, but he said they were unlucky and brought bad weather. They did. For a week after their arrival it blew a storm and poured rain. In a way it had its compensations. As the flooded rivers began to subside at last there were trout to be caught in plenty, trout with delicate pink flesh as well as the white variety, and salmon were being sold in Letterfrack and Clifden for half nothing.

Every mile of the long road from Clifden to Westport, surely the most beautiful in Ireland, is a constant joy to travel, though the country is miserably poor for anyone who might depend on it for a livelihood. Westport House is the seat of the Marquess of Sligo. It is open to the public and illustrates one of the mysteries of Irish economy; that however impoverished the life of the ordinary people, there was always room for a lord. During the

Galway Hooker (opposite). *At Cleggan you can buy your fish at the quayside straight from the boats.*

famine years of 1846 and 47, when over a million people died of hunger, hundreds of starving peasants knelt before the steps of Westport House to beg for help. Lord Sligo, to give him his due, did what he could, while the town of Westport and the country-side about, which are so peaceful and pretty to-day, witnessed scenes which horrified a young English observer called W. E. Forster:

'Westport was a strange and fearful sight; the streets crowded with gaunt wanderers, the men stamped with the livid mark of hunger, the children crying in pain. All the sheep were gone, all the cows, all the poultry killed—the very dogs had disappeared'.

While the lucky ones who could afford it fled to America or Canada, the rest died in their cabins among blighted fields.

It was in Connemara I rented a cottage from a man who, even in drink and among music making, carried an air about him which set him apart. The rent was modest, the cottage stood above a lake, lost in the hills and miles from anywhere. He was more interested in the company than the rent which, when it was paid to him each week, came back to the cottage fireside again in the shape of a bottle of whiskey. If I didn't finish it with him drink for drink, he would get offended. He used to travel down to the public house with me whenever I went that way and he thought a car was a marvellous thing to have, simply because the pub and the neighbours were too far away otherwise. One night, while we were sitting together over the weekly bottle of whiskey, he told me the cause of his melancholy. He said that at one time long ago his father and mother and six brothers and sisters lived together in that small cottage and were happy. Then one by one the others went to America and he was left alone with his father and mother. Then his father died. Then his mother. He was alone. At first he used to lie awake and alone at nights and prayed to his father and mother to talk to him. Nothing happened. He thought at first it was God who would not allow it, so he prayed to God to let one of them come to him, just for one brief moment. He asked God to have pity on his great loneliness. But nothing happened. Night after night he prayed and night after night in the silence between his prayers he heard nothing only the ticking of the clock and the creak of ash in the dying fire. Until one night it became so unendurable he rose again and dressed. Something drew him to the graveyard. He stood at the grave and entreated his mother and father to speak to him. Nothing happened; nothing stirred in the little graveyard; nothing at all. It was as he listened to the nothing-ness that made no response no matter how hard he implored and begged and wept, the thought for the first time came to him that there was nothing to beg from. He was talking to nothing. If God were there He would have let his mother or father come. If his father and mother were there they would have come in spite of God because they would have known how he was suffering and they loved him before everything. He did not blame God. He was not there. He did not blame his parents. They were not there either. In the graveyard that night he found out that beyond the little span of years granted to each man and woman there was only silence and emptiness. Instead of God and Heaven, there was only absence and a void.

That was the story he told me at his fireside in Connemara. He had worked it out long ago, he said, for right or for wrong and it set him apart. Greater than the lonely acres of bog and lake which surrounded him, was the loneliness squeezed into the little space of his heart.

9

Sinbad's Yellow Shore

ON a bright spring day in the year 1833, a sea captain named William Pollexfen piloted his sailing ship, The Dasher, past the metal man at Rosses Point on his way to Sligo Harbour. His background was mysterious and he was supposed by some to have been granted the freedom of a Spanish city, though which one no one seemed able to say and for what reason nobody quite knew. However, he settled in Sligo town, married a widow—a Mrs. Middleton—and in due course became the grandfather of W. B. Yeats, Ireland's greatest poet.

In the seventy-four years of his life, Yeats inspired the Irish Literary Revival, gave his country a National Theatre that became world famous and established himself as a poet regarded by many as the greatest of the 20th century. Despite all that, and the fact that he was honoured by being made a Senator of State, he fell under the stern disapproval of the Honour-and-Virtue school, possibly because while in the Senate he spoke in favour of divorce, or perhaps simply because he affected so unashamedly the poetic role, in his studied bearing, his mode of dress and his manner of speech. He had, of course, defended the official Abbey shockers: Synge's 'In The Shadow of the Glen' and 'The Playboy of the Western World' and later O'Casey's 'The Plough and The Stars' when he flung back at an infuriated audience which was threatening to wreck everything within sight:

'You have disgraced yourselves again. Once more you have rocked the cradle of genius. The fame of O'Casey is born tonight'.

He also assured them that O'Casey had achieved his *Apotheosis*. O'Casey confessed later, with his usual humanity and dry wit, that it was the first time he had ever heard the word and had to hurry home to his dictionary to find out if he was being praised or blamed.

Whatever the cause, Yeats' contribution to the new Ireland was denigrated and his work, with the exception of his celebrated Inisfree poem and a few sentimental attempts at ballads which had, for Yeats, an unusual hint of religiosity about them (such as 'Father O'Hart' and 'The Ballad of Father Gilligan') was largely ignored. It was the old story; it was patriotism to work within the narrow convention, to accept the idealisation of the honourable and virtuous Celt; but to reveal that the ancient heroes were beset by the old Adam, or that the heroines were less than totally honest and pure, was in the worst of bad taste. To suggest that the ordinary peasant had any share in those same weaknesses was downright villainy. Yet Yeats, in everything he did or thought, in his work for national freedom, in his praise of the men of 1916, in his love of Irish people and places and his attachment to memories of childhood and youth, was intensely Irish in every way and intensely proud of his Irish birthright. The fact that he was also a writer and a genius naturally set him apart from most of his countrymen, but that is of a different order. Perhaps the truth is that the Honour-and-Virtue school simply feared his honesty of thought and distrusted his decidedly unusual airs.

On holidays in Sligo in the 1870s, however, all Yeats' battles and heartbreak still lay ahead of him. He was simply a child who was much in love with the countryside and much in awe of William Pollexfen, his stern old grandfather, observing his odd ways unnoticed and storing up those details about him that were to be recollected later; that he had a great scar on his hand, for instance, made by a whaling hook, and in the diningroom he kept a cabinet with bits of coral in it and a jar of water from

the Jordan, for the baptising of his children. William Pollexfen was prosperous. Wine Street in Sligo housed the offices of his thriving shipping business. Every day, from the quaint glass and slated turret on the roof (it can still be seen) his telescope swept the bay as he marked the comings and goings of his ships. He was a man of mettle, who kept a hatchet at his bedside for burglars. He was strict too. Advised at the age of eighty to take a little stimulant for his health's sake, he refused: 'No', he said, 'I am not going to form a bad habit'. If asked by the family to read prayers, he puzzled Yeats the child by never selecting anything else except the shipwreck of St. Paul. When he walked daily down John Street to the Churchyard, as the boy often observed him to do, it was to supervise the building of his own tombstone in case (as he once explained) the builder might try to add some useless ornament. The young Yeats found it difficult not to confuse him with God.

Though he was born in Dublin in Georgeville (now No. 5) Sandymount Avenue, Yeats spent so much of his childhood in Sligo that it became his adopted home. Much of his inspiration came from its legends, its superb scenery, the country people and the sailors and fishermen whose conversation and stories fascinated him. Even the eccentricities of his many relatives, the Yeatses, the Pollexfens, the Middletons, fed both his imagination and his pride. There is so much of personal biography in Yeats' writing, so much reference to characters and places, so much reflection on the formative elements in his experience, that the streets of Sligo and the surrounding countryside have had a dimension added to them for anyone even moderately acquainted with his work.

To make up for the terrifying rectitude of old William Pollexfen, Yeats' paternal grandfather was gay and a little bit

Sligo Harbour (opposite above) . . . *on a bright spring day in the year 1833 William Pollexfen piloted his sailing ship,* The Dasher, *into Sligo Harbour.*

William Butler Yeats (opposite below). '*I have walked on Sinbad's yellow shore and never shall another hit my fancy.*'

disreputable. The son of the rector of Drumcliffe and himself a curate in the parish of Tullylush in Co. Down, he was so addicted to gaming parties and to the pleasures of the hunt that his unfortunate rector despaired of making any good of him.

'I had hoped for a curate', he complained, 'but they have sent me a jockey'.

John Butler Yeats, the son of the sporting curate, married Susan Pollexfen of Sligo in St. John's Church on 10th September 1863. W. B. Yeats was born of their union in 1865.

His summer holidays with old William Pollexfen were spent first at Merville, which has been much changed since, and later at Rathedmond to which William Pollexfen retired, a house which can be seen just outside the town on the road to Strand-hill. Opposite to it is Thornhill, the residence of George Pollexfen, also an eccentric: 'At Sligo, where I still went for my holidays, I stayed with my uncle, George Pollexfen . . . He had one old general servant and a man to look after his horse, and every year he gave up some activity, and found there was one more food that disagreed with him. Through winter to summer he passed through a series of woollens that had to be weighed.'

Uncle George, though odd enough to weigh his woollens, was nevertheless, a favourite with the boy. They went on expeditions together from Thornhill along Cumeen strand, under the shadow of Knocknarea, the legendary mountain topped by the huge burial cairn which is supposed to be the resting place of Connaught's great warrior queen, Maeve. Across the bay rose the shape of Ben Bulben, another legendary mountain where Diarmuid, the warrior hero, hunted the wild boar and was slain. Some miles further along the same road, in the village of Ballisodare, the family flour mills stand on the river bank where the water thunders over a series of falls in the last moments of its journey to the sea. From Paddy Flynn, a bright-eyed little man who lived in a leaky, one-roomed cabin in Ballisodare, Yeats got many of the stories which he later retold in *The Celtic Twilight*.

Another house which belonged to his Uncle George and at which he spent his holidays is Moyle Lodge, in the village at Rosses Point. It was a strange household in which his uncle devoted himself to the study of magic while the old servant, Mary Battle, who was a clairvoyante, reported omens and visions and helped him to analyse dreams. All this bizarre activity impressed the young Yeats so deeply that it was to have a permanent effect, and not always a happy one, on his work and thought; nevertheless, Rosses Point left him with simpler and more normal memories of childhood which he recollected afterwards with affection:

'When I look at my brother's picture *Memory Harbour*—houses and anchored ship and distant lighthouse all set close together as in some old map—I recognise in the blue-coated man with the mass of white shirt the pilot I went fishing with, and I am full of disquiet and of excitement, and I am melancholy because I have not made more and better verses. I have walked on Sinbad's yellow shore and never shall another hit my fancy'.

On the strand at Rosses Point, in the long summers of childhood, he gathered those memories which he afterwards described as fragmentary remembrances of the seven days of creation.

Also at Rosses Point, beneath the hotel, where the grasslands slope down to the sea and the metal man points out the navigable channel for shipping, stands *Elsinore*, the house of another uncle, Henry Middleton, a recluse who locked his gate on the world. It was unoccupied and falling into decay when I first found it, but since then a local rowing club have taken possession, so it may be saved for a while longer. It inspired the poem which contains the verses:

My name is Henry Middleton
I have a small demesne
A small forgotten house that's set
On a storm bitten green
I scrub its floors and make my bed
I cook and change my plate
The post and garden boy alone
Have keys to my old gate
From mountain to mountain ride the fierce horsemen

Though I have locked my gate on them
I pity all the young
I know what devil's trade they learn
From those they live among
Their drink, their pitch and toss by day
Their robbery by night
The wisdom of the people's gone
How can the young go straight
From mountain to mountain ride the fierce horsemen.

As the summers of boyhood and youth passed, time filled the
grave the old sailor had built in St. John's Churchyard in Sligo
town and to-day the names on the tombstone bring another of
his poems to the mind:

Five and twenty years have gone
Since old William Pollexfen
Laid his strong bones down in earth
By his wife Elizabeth
In the grey stone tomb he made
And after twenty years they laid
In that tomb by him and her
His son George, the Astrologer . . .

. . . At all these deaths women heard
A visionary, white seabird
Lamenting that a man should die
And with that cry I have raised my cry.

His mother, Susan Pollexfen, died in exile, but there is a brass
plaque in the Church erected to her memory by the family.

The ruins of Sligo Abbey, pillaged and burned in 1641 during
the sack of Sligo by Cromwell's troops, its White Friars
slaughtered in the light of the High Altar candles, its Abbot
facing the troopers with the great brass Crucifix held high over

Yeats' Grave, Drumcliffe Churchyard '. . . *Just my name and these
words* . . .'

Cast a cold Eye
On Life, on Death.
Horseman, pass by!

W. B. YEATS

June 13th 1865
January 28th 1939

his head, became for Yeats another symbol of Irish history and took its place among the folktales and the mythical Kings and Queens in the storehouse of his imagination. It was founded for the Dominican Order by the Earl of Kildare in 1252. The County Library and Museum, through the initiative of the Librarian, Miss Nora Niland, has in addition to its valuable collection of letters, photographs and first editions of W. B. Yeats' poems, an impressive collection of paintings by his equally famous brother Jack B. Yeats.

Some miles from Sligo town the road to Lissadell rides high above the magnificent sweep of Drumcliffe Bay, passing as it goes the entrance to the Churchyard of Drumcliffe, where Yeats himself is buried. An ancient Celtic cross and the stump of a Round Tower mark the access road. Old, branchy trees full of rooks reach almost as high as the Church, while the plain gravestone carries the epitaph he composed for himself. A short while before his death he had written to Ethel Mannin to say he was arranging about his burial:

'It will be in a little remote churchyard in Co. Sligo, where my great grandfather was the clergyman a hundred years ago. Just my name and the dates and these words:

Cast a cold eye
On life, on death
Huntsman, pass by.

But in the letter the word 'Huntsman' is struck out and the word 'Horseman' which is in the finished epitaph, has been substituted.

2

Ben Bulben, the legendary mountain, rises high above Yeats' resting place. It was the hunting ground once of the great heroes and the scene of the death of Diarmuid, who had earned the enmity of Fionn McCool by eloping with Grainne on the evening before she and Fionn were to be married. After living as an outlaw for sixteen years, pursued from place to place, Diarmuid made peace with Fionn and was allowed to return to his possessions. But Fionn still thought of vengeance and by a trick he involved Diarmuid in the hunt of an enchanted boar, one without ears or tail, on the slopes of Ben Bulben. Diarmuid killed the boar, but in the struggle, with a mighty spring, it wounded him mortally by ripping out his bowels. As he lay dying Fionn came and stood over him unpityingly.

'It would please me greatly, Diarmuid of the love-spot', he said, 'if the women of Ireland could see you now; for your beauty is turned to ugliness and your choice form to deformity'.

Diarmuid reminded Fionn of having rescued him from peril in their days of friendship and, knowing Fionn had the gift of healing any man with a draught of well water drawn in his two hands, begged him to do so.

'There is no well here', Fionn said.

'That is not true', Diarmuid said, 'only nine paces from you is the best well of prime water in the world'.

Fionn hesitated, but on the entreaty of Oscar and the rest of the Fianna, who recited to him many of the deeds done by Diarmuid in the old days, he at last went to the well. On his way back his resolution faltered and he let the water fall through his fingers. He went again, but again 'having thought upon Grainne' the water slipped away through his fingers. Oscar then confronted him and told him if he did not bring the water promptly this time either he or Oscar would not leave Ben Bulben alive. Fionn went a third time but it was too late. As he was returning Diarmuid died. They covered the body with their cloaks and took his hound back to Grainne so that she would know he had been slain.

Between Drumcliffe and Ben Bulben lies the scene of a battle from later history, the famous 'Battle of the Books' which was fought in 561 between the followers of St. Colmcille and St. Finian, over a psalter lent by Finian which Colmcille copied. The King of Ireland gave judgment that the copy also belonged to Finian on the principle 'to every cow its calf and to every book its copy'. Colmcille refused to accept this succinct summary of the principle of copyright law and held on to the copy. A bloody battle ensued.

Lissadell, the demesne of the Gore-Booth family, lies on the northern shore of Drumcliffe Bay, just beyond the small village of Carney. Yeats received his first invitation to make a visit in 1896, when he was just over thirty years of age. He became a close friend of the daughters of the house; Eva, a poetess and Constance, afterwards Countess Markiewicz. The elegance of life in the great classical house can be glimpsed from photographs in the Gore-Booth family album; Eva and Constance horse riding, or taking part in amateur theatricals; a first Ball dress; Constance painting: reflections of that selfsure culture of the Irish Protestant Ascendancy which looked so permanent and yet was about to collapse in ruins. The elegance was much to Yeats' taste, for he had leanings towards aristocratic imaginings about himself, based on the fact that the poets of ancient Ireland were accorded the rank of nobles and his own conviction that the practice of poetry endowed him of its nature with blueness of blood.

The grounds of Lissadell estate, with its wooded acres bordered by the sands of Lissadell Bay, are open to the public, as also is the house. Among the many exhibits is a painting by Sarah Purser of Eva and Constance as children. It catches their contrasting characters; Eva, gentle and diffident; Constance, who was to become an Irish heroine, strong and determined. Both girls left home at the beginning of the new century, Eva to take up social work in Manchester where she devoted herself almost entirely to women's suffrage and the organisation of exploited textile workers; Constance to Paris and the study of painting. While there she met and married Count Casimir de Markiewicz, also a painter. On her return she worked with Jim Larkin in the great Dublin Lock-out of 1913, when she helped in the food kitchens which were set up to feed the families of the workers. She also joined the Citizen Army and took part in the Rising of 1916. As one of the leaders she was condemned to death but later was reprieved because of her sex. By 1927

Ben Bulben (opposite above). *It was the hunting ground once of the great heroes and the scene of the death of Diarmuid.*

Landing a currach in the Aran Islands (opposite below).

both girls were dead. While Yeats was at Seville, during October and November of the same year, he wrote of them in his well known *In Memory of Eva Gore-Booth and Constance Markiewicz*.

> . . . Dear shadows, now you know it all
> All the folly of a fight
> With a common wrong or right
> The innocent and the beautiful
> Have no enemy but time.

Eva left a poem 'The little waves of Breffny' which very sensitively evokes the feeling of Sligo landscape:

The grand road from the mountain goes shining to the sea
And there is traffic in it and many a horse and cart
But the little roads of Cloonagh are dearer far to me
And the little roads of Cloonagh go rambling through my heart

A great storm from the ocean goes shouting o'er the hill
And there is glory in it and terror on the wind
But the haunted air of twilight is very strange and still
And the little winds of twilight are dearer to my mind

The great waves of the Atlantic sweep storming on the way
Shining green and silver with the hidden herring shoal
But the little waves of Breffny have drenched my heart in spray
And the little waves of Breffny go stumbling through my soul.

That 'haunted air of twilight' adds its aura of mystery to the beautiful area of Glencar, with its waterfalls and high precipices towering above the white-washed cottage in which Yeats spent a holiday with Arthur Symons; and the little waves of Breffny dance on Lough Gill at the foot of Breffny Hill. It was Inisfree, one of Lough Gill's many islands, that returned in memory to Yeats as he watched a coloured ball bobbing on a jet of water in

Thoor Ballylee (opposite). *Gort and Ballylee and Kiltartan in County Galway meant much to the mature Yeats.*

the window of a London shop, to become the poem which the whole world seems to know.

Yeats summed up his childhood attachment to Sligo in a passage in *Autobiographies* in which he describes his sister and he in London, talking together of their feelings of longing and heartbreak at the fountain in Holland Park:

'I know we were both very close to tears and remember with wonder—for I had never known anyone that cared for such mementoes—that I longed for a sod of earth from some field I knew, something of Sligo to hold in my hand.'

What he could not clasp in his hand, he held close in his heart; as a boy, as a youth, as a mature and dedicated poet. And when he lay dying at his hotel in Cap Martin in the south of France in January of 1939, he had already decided that Sligo earth would receive his body. Throughout the war years it rested in the hillside cemetery of Roquebrune, but when peace came the Irish Government brought him home and his wish was fulfilled. Although Gort and Ballylee and Kiltartan in County Galway meant much to the mature Yeats, and although Coole Park became a second home and its mistress, Lady Gregory, a second mother, in that final return to Sligo and the surroundings in which he had lived through his 'seven days of creation', both his work and his personality achieved completion.

10

By Way of Pilgrimage

IN Donegal I caught my first trout, encountered flying ants for the first time and watched the wasps one summer afternoon drowning in hundreds in a half empty jamjar, until it became a buzzing, wriggling, yellow-and-black-hooped cemetery. That was in childhood, on the shores of Gartan Lake. We had come from Letterkenny to Churchill on a narrow gauge railway (the Londonderry and Lough Swilly) a long pull uphill through thickly wooded country for the first few miles during which it was possible to pluck the hedge blossoms through the carriage windows while the engine, although making hardly any progress at all, puffed so much it nearly blew itself to bits. There were stops to chase wandering cows off the line or simply to give the engine time to gather its senses. The narrow gauge railway is now defunct, which is a great pity. It had lovable qualities.

The second time I went to County Donegal was by way of pilgrimage, for it is the home county of my mother's people. My great-great-grandmother, who lived to be nearly a hundred, was a Moran of Buncrana, a Presbyterian who had a grain store. During the Great Famine of 1846/47, I am glad to be able to say, she threw it open without charge to the starving people of the neighbourhood. It seems to have done her fortune no damage, because when she was well into her nineties she was still serving in the shop, with the help of her two unmarried daughters, who were themselves approaching their seventies. Whatever about the daughters, my great-great-grandmother, although her memory grew to be not quite the best, was not a woman to lose hope. If the daughters were in the back of the shop when an eligible traveller came in to do business, my great-great-grandmother never let the opportunity slip: 'Come out with you now, Agnes and Elsie', she would call out, 'and wish good-morning to Mr. Gallacher'.

Buncrana stands on the eastern shore of Lough Swilly, the longest sea inlet in Donegal which in the 1914–18 war sheltered The Grand Fleet. A few miles to the north of Buncrana are the forts of Dunree and Lenan Head, the last to be handed over to the Irish Government when the British gave back the defensive points they had retained in the key ports of the Republic. That was in October 1938, less than a year before the outbreak of the Second World War. De Valera refused to give them back, but undertook to man them against invasion. There was a story going round the Dublin pubs at the time that at a reception during the negotiations, De Valera asked Churchill what he would have and Churchill said he would like what he came for — a few ports.

Lough Swilly figures largely over a long stretch of Irish history. It is said to have got its name from a monster which lived in its depths in the 6th century called Suileach (from the Irish word Súil, meaning eye) which had hundreds of eyes festooning its head. It terrified the countryside until it was slain after a bloody fight by St. Colmcille. In 1587 the young Red Hugh O'Donnell was taken prisoner on Lough Swilly by a trick of Lord Deputy Perrot. At that time there was a Carmelite Monastery on the western shores of the lough near Rathmullen, at which a number of Donegal clans gathered each year for a short while to fulfil their religious duties. To while away the dull hours between devotions, no doubt, they brought along with them their staghounds and hunting gear. One day, while Red Hugh and his party were enjoying the chase, an invitation was brought to them to join the master of a ship which had just put in to trade in Spanish wines, in sampling his wares. When they got on board a party was in progress, with wine and music flowing. The hospitality was lavish and the hours passed. At last, when they rose to take their leave, they found their unsteadiness was not altogether the result of the wine. The ship had hoisted sail and was well under way. They were lodged in Dublin Castle as prisoners of the Queen, until they escaped with the help of Fiach McHugh O'Byrne of Wicklow on Christmas night four years later, to make their journey through the mountains of Wicklow in a blizzard to the safety of O'Byrne's stronghold in Glenmalure.

Red Hugh lived to lead his army in the battle of Kinsale. After his defeat there he set off for Spain to seek further help. He persuaded Philip to the point where orders were given and a force was assembled at Corunna for another invasion of Ireland, but for one policy reason or another it never sailed. Meanwhile the news from Ireland was of the collapse of Munster resistance, the destruction of Dunboy Castle and the incredible retreat of the broken O'Sullivan Beare described earlier. O'Donnell fell sick—one account says he was poisoned by a nail in a pair of boots given him as a present by an English agent—and died in September of 1602. The Great O'Neill also saw his last of Ireland from Lough Swilly when the Flight of the Earls took place in 1607.

Almost two centuries later Admiral Bompart sailed for Lough Swilly from Brest with a French fleet and 3,000 troops aboard. Wolfe Tone, who had persuaded the French Directory to lend French aid to the United Irishmen, was in command of one of the frigates, the Hoche. But they were engaged by a British squadron off Tory Island and forced to surrender. Tone was marched with the rest through the streets of Buncrana. One account says he was unnoticed because of his French uniform until he himself disclosed his identity to Sir George Hill at Buncrana Castle; another that Sir George, who had been his contemporary during college days, deliberately betrayed him by stepping forward to shake his hand, saying: 'My dear Tone . . .'

He was courtmartialled and sentenced to be hanged, but at least escaped that indignity by cutting his own throat while lodged in Newgate gaol. Tone was one of the most attractive

Wolfe Tone . . . *one of the most attractive personalities of the United Irish Movement.*

personalities of the United Irish Movement; young, witty, with an intensely human side to his natural nobility which shines through his diaries. He was a bad performer on the flute but passionately fond of music. During his long sojourn on the Continent petitioning for help for the Irish cause he passed much of the time playing sonatas with one of the Admirals. His estimate of his own standard of performance he sets down in one honest word: *execrable.*

Something of his character is caught in an account in his diaries of an early attempt at invasion (1796) in which he took part, but which had to be abandoned because of violent storms after the fleet had stood off Bantry Bay for some days:

December 25
'Last night I had the strongest expectations that today we should debark, but at two this morning I was awakened by the wind. I rose immediately and wrapping myself in my greatcoat, walked for an hour on the gallery, devoured by the most gloomy reflections. The wind continues right ahead, so that it is absolutely impossible to work up to the landing place, and God knows when it will change. The same wind is exactly favourable to bring the English upon us, and these cruel delays give the enemy time to assemble his entire force in this neighbourhood; and perhaps (it is, unfortunately, more than perhaps) by his superiority in numbers, in cavalry, in artillery, in money, in provisions, in short in everything we want, to crush us . . . If we are taken my fate will not be a mild one; the best I can hope for is to be shot as an *emigré rentré,* unless I have the good fortune to be killed in Action; for most assuredly if the enemy will have us, he must fight for us. Perhaps I may be reserved for a trial, for the sake of striking terror into others, in which case I shall be hanged as a traitor and embowelled etc. . . . As to the embowelling, *"je m'en fiche"*, if ever they hang me, they are welcome to embowel me if they please. These are pleasant prospects . . .'

He lingered for a week in great pain with his self-inflicted wound because he had only succeeded in partly severing the windpipe. Once, while half conscious, he heard the surgeon who was attending him saying to another that there might be a possibility of his recovering. Tone opened his eyes, smiled and said 'I am sorry to have been so bad an anatomist'.

Sir George Hill, the college contemporary to whom he had surrendered at Buncrana, wanted him executed immediately. When told the delay was due to the fact that if Tone were moved he would die almost immediately, his comment was merciless: 'Then I would have sewed up his neck and finished the business', he said.

When I was at school there was a play called *The Eagle of the North* which was so highly regarded for its sound patriotic and religious content by the good Brothers who taught us that every other year it was trotted out for the annual Christmas end-of-term concert. It concerned the capture of Red Hugh O'Donnell at Lough Swilly, his incarceration with Henry and Art O'Neill in Dublin Castle and his escape and eventual return to his people in Donegal. Although I played the part of Henry O'Neill in one of these plays I have only the haziest recollection of the action; possibly because during the blizzard scene on the mountainside, around about the end of the second act, and in which Art O'Neill dies (attended, as I remember, by the ministrations of angelic visitors), Henry wanders off into the storm and opts out of the action altogether. What I have had cause to remember all my life, however, is the prison scene of the night of Christmas 1591, in which the action required the three of us, in the candle-lit gloom of our cell, to lift up each other's spirits with songs about home. This was the music bit, mandatory in all amateur presentations of the time, and as was usual in those days, the author was having no damned nonsense about musical authenticity or the use of period airs; he wanted stuff that was going to get across directly to the hearts of the fathers and mothers in the audience.

What Art sang I can't remember, but Red Hugh obliged with *Green Inishowen* and, as Henry, my contribution, helped by an unseen and deplorably anachronistic piano, was *The Hills of Donegal*. It is a difficult song with an unusually wide range and a death trap for the nondescript singer who can easily start it too high. Yet it has dogged me through life since. My mother adored it, not simply because I was heard by everybody to sing it from the stage, but because it moved her with proud memories of her parents and her birthplace. She had me singing it at parties and on visits to relatives and on every other occasion conceivable. Despite all that, the words of the second verse are effective in a curious way, in that they never fail to evoke the landscape and the nestling houses whenever I hear them sung—by someone else.

I mind the waiting valleys that light up at dawn of day
And I mind the dawnlight creeping on the rugged crests of grey
And I mind the linnets singing as the dark clouds lift and go
And the grey hills send the sunshine to the waiting hearts below
To the waiting hearts
Below . . .

The words went round and round in my head as I free-wheeled down the steep descent of the road to Ardara between the high shoulders of Glengesh and Crocknapeast. For that is how it was: not exactly the dawnlight but the morning anyway; a wild and spreading valley, a river gleaming at the bottom of the steep fall to the right of the road, sunlight on the mountain peaks and cloud shadows chasing along their sides, the faint smell of burning turf in the air, and birdsong. I was eighteen years of age, riding the first three-speed bicycle I had ever possessed, alone and on pilgrimage with the sum of four pounds ten in my pocket to keep me for fourteen days. I had stuck a sprig of heather in the handlebars for luck. If I close my eyes I see the delicate, purple bloom, the silver flash of spokes, the road ribboning swiftly backwards under the wheels.

In the public house at Ardara there was music in session. Every third or fourth customer had a fiddle or a tin whistle or a melodeon. There had been, or there was about to be, a Feis. An old man who was holding court among a group of non-players, asked me:

'Have you music?'

'A little', I said, 'but my grandfather had more'.

'And who was he?'

'Tom Cannon', I said, 'from this town of Ardara'.

183

'Had he a brother Henry?'

'He had', I said, 'and another called James'.

The old man stood up and shook my hand.

'He was a good friend of mine in years gone by'. He put his arm about my shoulder to guide me to the windows.

'The Cannons used to live in a house across the road there', he said, 'but they pulled it down and there's a Bank in its place now'.

I thanked him for the information and felt the Bank touch added distinction. I had been very fond of my grandfather. He was the one who used to lapse into Irish when his emotions got the better of him. In calmer moments he made violins which he either gave away or lent to friends and never got back.

'I'll tell you more than that', said my friend, 'I knew your great-grandfather. He was old Henry Cannon of Dunkineely; a tall man, with a long white beard and a straight back—a cooper by trade'.

'My grandfather', I said, 'was a carpenter. Do you remember that he played the fiddle?'

'They all played the fiddle', the old man said, 'but the best of the lot was Harry—when he put his mind to it'.

'How so?'

'In this way. He was a man who could turn his hand too easily to anything and the result of that is a kind of unpredictability. You may not know that now, but it's a judgement you'll come to when you're a bit longer in this world. Did you know your Uncle Harry was in great demand on certain occasions?'

'I did not'.

'On the birth of twins', the old man said. 'As you may know, the dilemma with twins is—what do you do about the cradle. Your Uncle Harry was the first man to find the answer. He invented a double cradle for twins and you'll find his work still in odd corners of the county'.

We sat down again. In a short while, being a visitor, I was asked for a song. Not for the first time in this life, my Christian Brothers education stood to me. I gave them *The Hills of Donegal*.

At Gartan, beyond the village of Churchill, is the birthplace of St. Colmcille. It may be signposted now, but in those days it meant making enquiries at a gate lodge, to the left of the road, where it leaves the lakeside and climbs above the valley on its right and then a lengthy enough cycle ride into remote mountain territory. A modern Celtic cross stands among nondescript ruins. He was born in the year 561 and the event was marked by the usual expressions of divine interest. An Angel showed a beautifully embroidered cloak to his mother, Eithne, who thought at first it was for her. However, the angel took it back, spread it in the wind and let it float slowly away over the lake and the hills. As they watched it Eithne knew it was her son who would soon be born and who would travel far and wide for Christ. Colmcille's ruined oratory, about half a mile further north is still a place of veneration, where pilgrims seeking his intercession leave tokens of their visit on the remnant of the altar. The offerings are strange—coins, combs, medals, rings, fragments of personal clothing—and they embody a faith which is still very close to the superstitions and beliefs of the early Irish church.

Also near Gartan, on the roadside above the lake between Glendowan and Churchill there is another relic of Colmcille legend—if you can find it. It is a slab of natural rock known as Leac na Cumhaidh, the Stone of Sorrowing, or more accurately, the stone of homesickness or nostalgia. When Colmcille was leaving Ireland to go into perpetual exile, he sat on it to rest and grieve and since then Donegal emigrants (many of them seasonal workers going to Scotland) used to stop there to pray as they passed along the road on their way to the boat at Derry.

The cult of Colmcille seems to have formed much of the religious life pattern of Donegal and is extraordinarily persistent. Once, in Barnes Gap, a man who was talking to me invited me to delay a few minutes longer to see the Black Pig running through the gap as Colmcille had foretold. It was one of the Saint's many prophecies of the signs and wonders which would signify the near approach of the end of the world. In a few minutes it happened. There was a low rumbling in the distance and after a while one of the little engines of the Londonderry

& Lough Swilly Railway crossed the viaduct which spans the gap, grunting and snorting and breathing fire and smoke as it went. It was, we both acknowledged, an impressive demonstration of the saint's foresight. The viaduct is in ruins to-day and the Black Pig has gone back to its cronies in the underworld.

Glenveagh Estate, to the west of Gartan, occupies one of the loneliest and most beautiful areas of Donegal. The 25,000 acres of mountain and lake which surround its castellated mansion have been compared more than favourably with Killarney. The first time I saw the Castle, which in its lake and mountain setting looks like something out of an historical romance, was by a trick. The grounds were private and visitors were not welcome, but a sympathetic grocer solved the problem by suggesting I should borrow the shop's messenger bike and deliver a batch of bread which was expected. I did so. It was evening by then and almost an hour of the journey was over a rough mountain track, with patches of woodland at intervals. Mist was stealing down the mountain slopes, the lake was grey and ominous, its surface wrinkled like the face of an old witch; in the woods the evening silence had stilled all movement. Seen against the greyness of lake and mist, the castle looked unreal, an enchanted image likely to dissolve as one drew nearer. However, it remained there long enough for me not only to deliver the bread, but to take a further order for sugar and flour, the exact quantity of which I entered in my notebook. On the road back I was benighted and got caught in a thunderstorm. Picking my way by the tiny light of the bicycle lamp and expecting to be blown into one of the flooded dykes at any moment, I wondered if the storm might be God's judgement on those who delude their betters.

The mountain land all around Glenveagh once supported a thriving community but in 1861 the landowner, John George Adair, cleared out the whole population and razed their cabins to the ground, mainly because they got in the way of his shooting. He was the son of a wealthy landowner in Leix who, when he bought the estate in 1857, is said to have had philanthropic notions regarding his tenants. Unfortunately a dispute arose when some of the peasants challenged his right to shoot over certain areas. He was an arrogant man, prepared to go to any lengths to establish his overlordship even where, strictly speaking, its writ did not run. In the end the affair became so bitter that a battalion of soldiers and two hundred police were drafted into the area and, on John Adair's orders, every single house of a community that had been living there for generations was destroyed. A local committee with the assistance of the Government helped to obtain free emigration to Australia for many of the dispossessed, which relieved some from actual starvation but did nothing to ease the bitterness. The area is now the haunt of hundreds of wild deer. Tragedy still lingers over these beautiful and empty acres and in the verses of a peasant ballad *Cruel John Adair* which commemorates the clearances:

> He brought the sheriff to our doors
> He quenched our fires so bright
> My grandsire he is no more
> He died that fatal night;
> My mother weeps her youngest child,
> A boy of beauty rare,
> But four months old, so meek and mild;
> All done by John Adair
>
> For many a year our weary race
> Have tilled the mountain side;
> Have smoothed Glenveagh's old rugged face
> Have steamed the Atlantic wide;
> Full fifty homes he has levelled all,
> And wild sighs fill the air;
> Full fifty thousand curses fall
> On cruel John Adair.

When I first travelled the secondary roads from Lough Veagh to Rosguill by way of the village of Glen, they were rough enough to make the going backbreaking in places. Yet what was lost by way of comfort was made up for in isolation, in the feeling of having come at last into a world set apart for travellers who worked hard at their job. The road winding along the shore of Glen lake gave glimpses of Muckish, a pagan

An Eviction. '*He brought the sheriff to our doors*
He quenched our fires so bright . . .'

mountain if ever there was one. The pub in the village itself was whitewashed and lamplit. Beyond it, somewhere in the flat, sandy wastes of the Rosguill peninsula, there was a cottage which gave me shelter for the night. It stood on the shores of an eternally ebbed sea, surrounded by sandhills, lost and lonely in a wilderness of tall sand grass. An elderly woman opened the door and asked me in to rest when I looked for directions. She was living alone with her grandson in a place that could well pass for the last corner of the world, but she had the grace and courtesy which are the characteristics of the people of the country. While the grandson and I chatted the table was laid and tea was ready. After that we had some music, the grandson playing the melodeon and myself coaxing what tone I could out of a fiddle which he had made out of a soapbox. It was uncouth enough to look at, but it worked, to the extent at least of providing three isolated people with a night of unique enjoyment, which went on and on until there was no alternative, even if I had wished one, but to make my bed by the fireside. There are times when I have wondered if that cottage and that elderly woman and young man, that strangely shaped instrument and the memory of playing it, could possibly be real. I have looked since for the turn I took off the road all those years ago without ever finding it, but that proves nothing. There are lamplit pubs I once knew and hotels where you carried a candle with you to bed which I will never find again either.

The area around Rosapenna, apart from its golf course and its reputation for good fishing, is remarkable for swallowing up houses. In the eighteenth century several farms disappeared forever under shifting sands. More recently a Captain Stewart lost his house in the same circumstances. The story is that he ignored warnings from the locals about interfering with the sand grass around his property and had it cut and exported as fodder for cavalry horses during the 1914–18 war. The result was that the sand eventually smothered his house up to the top storey and when the furnishings had to be sold, the auctioneer conducted the sale sitting on the roof. Rosguill, stretching northwards of Rosapenna, was the end of my first journey through Donegal. It is deservedly famed for its wide beaches and the dramatic views from the road skirting the cliff high above them, an eight mile roundabout with the Atlantic beating against the breached rocks and the fissures smoking with great jets of foam. To the west of Rosguill, Horn Head, a black and massive bulwark, seems only a stone's throw away, especially when you look at it on an early morning when the air is clear, but the Atlantic has cut a long inlet for itself between them and it is a good day's cycle run through territory wild with mountain and sea from one peninsula to the other. Beyond Horn Head, nine miles or so from the mainland rises Tory Island. Like Aran, it is Irish speaking. Its two hundred inhabitants live in two villages, East Town and West Town. There are no rats on Tory, or so the story goes and I am told that people from the mainland collect earth from the island to rid their houses of infestation. Need I add that the man who banished the rats was Colmcille, who founded a monastery there.

2

Geographically, Donegal has always tended to be cut off from the rest of the country. It was the last considerable stronghold of the old Gaelic civilisation, which remained intact there until the defeat of O'Neill and the Flight of the Earls at the beginning of the 17th century. Its grip on old religious customs and beliefs has been just as tenacious, manifesting itself in ancient forms of veneration which, when you witness them, bring you back to the borderlands of Paganism and Christianity, the conjunction (in Ibsen's phrase) of The Old Beauty and The New Truth. Doon Well, in the parish of Gartan, is a striking example. Its history goes back to sometime in the 15th century, when a holy man named O'Friel was famed in the area for his power as a healer. Tradition has it that before his death he passed on his powers by blessing the waters of the well. Stories of cures circulated and still persist and emigrants take bottles of the water with them on their journeys. The well is located in boggy land under Carraig a'Duin, the crag which was the inauguration stone of the O'Donnells and on which Red Hugh was proclaimed Chief. On the capstone and tied about the bushes which surround the well are the usual supplicatory mementoes of the pilgrims. Anything or everything seems to do, for apart from coins and medals and rings, there are bandages tied about the bushes, pieces of coloured silk, hairpins, the blade of a penknife, beads and broken combs. The souvenir booklet sets out the devotional routine.

Doon Well
Prayers of the Station
Repeat Our Father and Hail Mary five times and
Apostles' Creed for your intention
Repeat same for each bottle of water
Our Father and Hail Mary for Father O'Friel
who founded it
Our Father and Hail Mary for Father Gallagher
who blessed it

Our Father and Hail Mary for the person who
put the shelter around it.

The well is still visited with reverence and devotion; the
people kneel, pray, drink its waters and fill their bottles to take
the water to their homes.

At Glencolumbkille, on the south-western coast, I've seen
Father McDyer lead his flock in the June pattern of the Patron
Saint, a barefooted journey around the remains of a monastic
cross and by rough boreens to places made holy by their
associations. In Donegal, more than elsewhere perhaps, people
tend to stick to the old ways. But custom, however deeply
rooted and scenery, however picturesque, are unlikely to satisfy
younger people in the world to-day unless moderate standards
of living and social and recreational opportunities are available
to them in addition. The journey from Donegal town to
Glencolumbkille, by way of Dunkineely, Killybegs and Kilcar
is a sequence of Donegal scenery at its best, a coastal road for
much of the way, with views across the airy width of Donegal
Bay and, when it bends inland, of great mountain shapes and
rivers that wind through heather and rock strewn valleys. The
journey is a delight, but for those who live on the coast at its
western extremity it is also a formidable barrier to easy communication with the rest of the country.

As a result, when Father McDyer came to Glencolumbkille he
found emigration bleeding it to death. During ten years
previously spent in England, including the war years, he had
worked among Irish emigrants and understood the tragedy
involved for many of them. In Glencolumbkille, with its
population of about 900 people and its 220 homes, 25 to 30 had
been leaving annually since after the famine. There was no
electricity when he first came, no water scheme and only one
tarmacadamed road. The natural resources were meagre too,
poor land averaging eight acres per holding with half of it
unarable.

If each holding was uneconomic on its own, Father McDyer
decided, co-operative farming might provide the answer. At

first, when one hundred and twenty of the farmers agreed to operate a commune, the Ministry of Agriculture disapproved. There were others too, who took alarm at the flavour of his ideas, which they regarded as ideologically suspect. However, being a sensible man with more regard for his people's welfare than the niceties of political theory he pushed ahead, so that to-day Glencolumbkille has a canning factory, a machine knit factory, metal craft and a building co-operative in addition to organised homecrafts in handknitting and crochet. For tourists there is a folk museum and a holiday village of 15 houses traditional in design but with modern amenities, which were built with local skills and labour and are let out to visiting families in the season. The roads have been improved and there is electricity and a public water scheme. The sad thing is that Father McDyer's reward for laying the foundations for a moderately comfortable and stable community has been, for the most part, suspicion and even bitter opposition. Officialdom, which for years was prepared to leave Glencolumbkille to rot in its isolation, suspects him of wanting to lower an Iron Curtain when all he is trying to do is to burst a way through the Green One. I am reminded of the words of Peadar O'Donnell on the limitations of the Irish Independence movement as it developed after 1916. Describing its mode of political thought O'Donnell said: 'The economic framework and social relationships . . . were declared outside the scope of the Republican struggle; even the explosive landlord-tenant relationship, and rancher-small farmer tension. The Republican movement was inspired by "pure ideals". In the grip of this philosophy the Republican struggle could present itself as a democratic movement of mass revolt without any danger to the social pattern; without any danger to the haves from the have-nots . . . under the shelter of pure ideals the Irish middle-class held its place within a movement it feared.'

What the Irish middle-class wanted was a revolution without

The Skelligs (opposite). *I felt I not only looked upon something unique but, by some trick of angle and light perhaps, something which had revealed to me the essence of a civilisation.*

social change and to a large extent that is what they succeeded in getting. As Parnell said on seeing the roadmender at work: 'Whether I'm elected or not, he'll still break stones'.

3

Peadar O'Donnell was born in Dungloe in the district known as the Rosses, a rocky, lake strewn area in the north west of Donegal, with fine beaches. As a young man he taught school on the islands off the coast, at a time when a great part of the island population migrated annually in the season for work as potato pickers in the tatie fields of Scotland. They went in squads that were family groups which often included twelve year old children. During one season, when there was talk of a strike of the potato workers, Peadar changed his schoolmaster's suit for working clothes and went off to Ayrshire to help to organise them if it should be necessary. He bedded down on straw, under musty Army blankets, resenting (as he confessed himself) everything around him and even angry with the workers for being passive in the face of such deplorable conditions. And then, one sleepless night 'with men and women, boys and girls, family groups asleep around me, my imagination kindled, and in those people who came as close to me as my own breath, I saw a remnant of the Irish of history, heroically holding on to homes in Ireland. My allegiance, loyalty, obsession, call it what you will, with that large and respectable section of the Irish people— the wage earners—had its roots in that experience and was enriched later by working as an organiser in the Trade Union movement.'

His association with island life gave him his best book, *Islanders*, which was set among the simple community of Inishkeeragh. That little island has long been abandoned, but I remember journeying back to it with him while touring The Rosses in the 1960s, setting out from Burtonpoint in Philly Boyle's boat. It was a fine day at the height of the fishing season. The catches were good; everyone was in the best of humour. A whitewashed slogan on the cliff face of Rutland Island, the nearest to the mainland, had been written by a football enthusiast for the benefit of travellers.

Up Arran Rovers

So far as Rutland was concerned, there were only Hughie McCole and his sister, the last two people on the island, left to respond to it. Hughie earns his livelihood fishing and enjoys his isolation, having turned down the offer of a house on the mainland.

'I have the whole island to myself', he said, 'to do what I like with and go where I please'.

'And where are the neighbours now?' Peadar asked.

'All scattered. Some in Burtonport and others in America and some in the graveyard which is the end of us all'.

'And what about Inishkeeragh and Easter Island?'

'All bought up', Hughie said, 'by the French and the English and people from Belfast. There's some of them for putting up "Private" notices'.

'You don't agree with "Private" notices, Hughie?'

'It's unneighbourly and a thing was never heard of in Donegal. It'll bring an ill feeling. But maybe the I.R.A. boys'll get after them and put a bit of manners on them'.

'And the fishing Hughie—how is that?'

'I'll tell you this, Peadar, it's not so good', Hughie said, 'because there's no good boatmen left. Only fellows with them hardy-gurdies stuck on the sterns of their boats to churn up the water and frighten the fish'.

'You'd rather have the oars?'

'I'd rather have the oars anyday. An oar has saved many a man's life'.

We walked the derelict island along a single street of empty houses. The schoolhouse was bolted and padlocked, the grass covered the paving stones. Smoke from a solitary chimney marked the only kitchen where life continued as Hughie's sister went about her housework.

In Arranmore, three miles out from Burtonport and the largest of the islands, things were livelier ('noisier', they say locally). A football team, Arran Rovers presumably, was at practice on the strand, probably the only soccer team in the

Peadar O'Donnell. *His association with island life gave him his best book,* Islanders.

world whose players shout at one another in Irish. The island, with about 900 inhabitants, has its hotels and public houses and a summer school for students of the Irish language but the population is slowly dwindling there too. The pull of the mainland and the attractions of living in America are strong.

Inishkeeragh, about two miles to the south of Arranmore, was entirely forsaken. We made the journey, in spite of Hughie McCole's scathing condemnation of hurdy-gurdies, in a boat with an outboard engine. There was nothing on the island it could disturb anyway, except the silence. You could almost touch the silence. A boat with a great gaping hole in its side lay rotting above the pier. Beyond it a street of low houses stood roofless and windowless. A water pump had toppled and lay rusting. Weeds and coarse grass had taken over the street. We stood for a while outside the empty schoolhouse where Peadar had begun his adult career over fifty years before. It had inspired him to write *Islanders* while in prison and awaiting sentence of death for his political activities, a time when he believed his own life was on short lease but that the sheltered and happy life described in his novel would go on. Life reversed the picture. He stood in silence on that summer day, a man in his middle seventies with undiminished vigour of mind, and contemplated the wreckage of an island and a way of life that had consoled him in his solitude. It is understandable that he should speak with bitterness of the neglect which has allowed the slow death of the islands of Gweebarra Bay and the mountain town-lands of the Rosses.

'These broken down islands, these mountain townlands were, most sharply, *my* Ireland. I had moved around them in the Black and Tan days and again after my escape from prison. The people of these townlands had given themselves over to the independence struggle; indeed, had exhausted themselves in it. I brought a column of men, the First Active Service Unit, into West Donegal and there is scarcely a house there that at one time or another did not give them shelter. I came to one of them myself at four o'clock one morning, having been wounded on the side of Glendowan Hill and I was nursed and protected. But the nation that had used them to loosen the British overlordship turned its back on them and left them to perish painfully, house by house.'

The people of Inishkeeragh had left the usual bits and pieces of their property behind them; broken crockery, bent fire irons, kettles and three legged pots that were now eaten and brown with rust. They were called 'Bastible' pots by the old people, a corruption of the name 'Barnstable', where they were manufactured. I wandered off to examine them and found in one of the houses a little donkey. At first, in the gloom, I thought he must surely be alive, for there was no sign at all of wasting or corruption. He was standing at one end of an abandoned iron bedstead and when my eyes got used to the light I could see what had happened. He had poked his head between the bars of the bed-end and had been unable to free himself. Trapped and held prisoner and with no human being at hand to help, he had starved to death. How many years before, I wondered, and through how many days and nights of slow agony.

We chugged our way back to the mainland in evening light across a placid sea. The sun laid a long track on the water. It lit up the great mountain masses to the east and to the south. Peadar sat silent, withdrawn, a man growing old—if men such as he can ever be said to grow old—with that ever deepening understanding of the inner and outer worlds which is a man's final triumph and completion.

I did not tell him about the donkey. It was not the moment. I thought of it though, its little neck caught in the bars, dead and alone on the empty island and the night coming down.

II

Old Bones on the Mountain

WHEN I think of County Meath, I think first, for it is nearest in history, of the bridge across the river at the little village of Slane and the plaque which commemorates the birth of the poet Francis Ledwidge, who died in the First World War. Or I think of the ruins of Dunmoe Castle near Donaghmore on the road to Slane, set high above one of the most picturesque stretches of the Boyne. I can never look at it without a couplet from God knows where coming automatically to mind.

> O, who'll be king I do not know
> But I'll be D'Arcy of Dunmoe

Or I think of Oldbridge near the village of Donore, not because the Battle of the Boyne at which William III defeated James II and about which extreme Orangemen are still exulting, was fought there on 12th July 1690, but because of a story the writer Mary Lavin once told me about it. As a young girl she was conducted along the Boyne walk by the Abbey dramatist Brinsley MacNamara, a rare privilege indeed. As they were about to cross the bridge at Oldbridge they were stopped by a young soldier who was on guard.

'I'm afraid I can't let you cross the bridge, sir', said the soldier.

'And why not?' asked Brinsley, who was large, portly and

had a grand manner.

'Because, sir, we're on manoeuvres and it's just been blown up by an imaginary explosion'.

'Then stand aside, young man', Brinsley commanded in his gravest manner, 'this young lady and I are in an imaginary boat'.

Meath, say the guide books, is a rich limestone plain, broken in the north west by the Loughcrew hills. It is a lot more. Pagan and early Christian Kings ruled here for centuries. It was the seat of the High Kings; it is at the centre of most of the ancient stories. All the early and magic-working races one glimpses through the shifting mists of Irish pre-history took up residence and fought out their battles for survival or supremacy here; the Firbolgs (the little dark men), the Tuatha de Danaan (tall and fair), the Milesians. It was their Royal and sacred burial ground, dotted to-day with their great tumuli, their passage graves, their megalithic monuments.

> The host of great Meath were buried
> In the middle of lordly Brugh,
> The great Ulster kings used to bury
> At Taillten with pomp

Meath was at the centre of Irish history. St. Patrick lit his Pascal fire on Slane Hill; the Danes raided and devastated; the Normans built their castles and left their mausoleums and their knightly effigies. The Reformation stripped its monasteries, the Cromwellians terrorized it and sold its men and women into slavery. On the Boyne the Irish army of James II suffered its defeat and English conquest was complete—or almost. In 1798 the shattered insurgents retired symbolically to Tara and there made their last stand and were slaughtered. When Daniel O'Connell organised the Catholics to demand repeal, he chose Tara for his monster rally in 1843 and half a million of them assembled there. Yet Meath is more than an open air museum, for in a museum things are seen apart from their setting and their place of growth, whereas in Meath the remnants and reminders abide in the grasslands and by the roadways that the feet of the builders and the generations since then have walked;

Loughcrew Cairn. *A bronze age people with funeral music and pagan ritual piled a cairn above its kings.*

they breathe-in life among the colours of the landscape, suffering all weathers, surrounded by earth and light and air and water, those elements that are the nearest to the eternal this world will ever know.

Most of all, if I think of Meath, I think of those Loughcrew hills and the great, bronze-age burial mound on the summit of Sliabh na Caillighe, their highest peak. It is only about 900 feet or so, but it dominates the whole central plain. Ollamh Fodhla, one of the first of the pagan kings, who reigned over three thousand years ago, is said to be buried there. The ordinary people found their own explanation for the several mounds that lie in the area surrounding it. They blamed the Hag of Beara, an old crone who was something of a nuisance. She went hopping from hill to hill (the people say) with her apron full of rocks which she kept letting fall, so that they landed here, there and elsewhere all over the rich land of Meath. So they called the hill Sliabh na Caillighe—The Hill of the Hag.

One summer's evening, on my way down from the summit, I passed another man on his way to the top and sat down to watch him until he too, in his turn, stood against the skyline on the highest point of the ancient burial mound. I knew what he could see. I knew the great spread of the plain, its patterns, its lakes, its rich debris of countless centuries. I knew what was flowing into him and swamping his senses from the earth and air about him, so acutely that in the end I was not sure whether the figure on the cairn was not myself. Ultimately a country means more to its children than the observation of its fauna and flora, its average mean temperature, its annual rainfall, even the details of its history. It is an indivisible relationship and it speaks in the blood. There was some particle of that man in myself; some fragment of me in him.

A man, I thought, does not make himself—he is made. A man does not motivate his own impulses, nor does he condition his own responses, or forge his own truth. If there is individual uniqueness, it is the uniqueness of a link in a chain. A man is his own father and mother and his forebears. He is his own children and the generations that are yet to come. He is what his native earth makes of his body when it gives him to eat and what his native landscape offers to his spirit when it cries out for revelation. He responds, alike, to songs that were sung before his birth and to a music that is yet to be made. There is a sense in which there is neither past nor future—all is Present. So it is that all high places are the same high place and each tomb is every tomb.

There, where the wind flattens the grasses at the summit of the hill, a bronze age people with funeral music and pagan ritual piled a cairn above its kings. And because they did so, the man who climbs the hillside to-day still feels the presence of kings and ritual in the airs that blow about him. Are they dead—those old kings? If there is a death to be venerated, one wonders, is it not, perhaps, one's own?

He stood silently on the cairn, outlined against the evening sky, long cloud shadows moving slowly across the slopes. Who now stands in contemplation above the great plain, I wondered; the man—or the kings? Whose bones lie in that ancient earth; those of the kings—or of the man?

Index

Compiled by Susan Chesters

Index

Index

O'Connor, Frank, 15, 48, 82, 107
  and Irish monasticism, 94–100
  his stories of Cork, 111–116
  his translation of Brian Merriman's *The Midnight Court*, 127
O'Dea, Jimmy, 73
O'Donnell, Red Hugh
  Prince of Donegal, 91, 144, 178–9, 182
O'Donnell, Peadar, 193–5, 197–8
O'Faolain, Sean
  and society of Thirties, 23
  attacks false piety in *The Bell*, 48–50
  King of the Beggars, 118
O'Flaherty family, 134
O'Flaherty, Liam, 135, 136, 138
O'Friel, Father, 190
O'Higgins, Kevin, 37, 73
O'Kane, countrie of, 141
O'Leary, John, 16
O'Neill, Art, 182
O'Neill, Henry, 182
O'Neill, The Great, 32, 118, 139, 141–50, 179, 190
O'Rorke, 122
O'Sullivan Beare, 120–2, 179
O'Toole family, 83
O'Toole, Laurence, 84
Oldbridge, 199
Ollamh Fodhla, 201
Ormonde, Duke of, 68
Orwell Park, Dublin, 79
Oscar, 171
Ossian, 71–2
Ota, 107
Otway, Reverend Caesar, 88
Oughterard, 159

Parnell, Charles Stewart, 82
Patrick, controversy of the two saints, 97
Perrott, Sir John (later Lord Deputy), 178
Philip II of Spain, 144–5, 148, 179
Phoenix Park, Dublin, 68
Pitt, William, 28
Pine Forest, 70
Playboy of the Western World, The (J. M. Synge), 80, 162
Plough and the Stars, The (Sean O'Casey), 162
Plunkett, Lord, 89
le Poer, Eustace, 82–3
Pollexfen, George, 166
Pollexfen, Susan, 166, 168
Pollexfen, William, 162, 163, 165, 166
Portland, 121

Post Office rebellion, 36
Poulaphouca, 82
Power, Albert, 154
Power's Distillery, 54
Powerscourt House, 82, 92
Priscian, 105
Protestantism
  urged by English in 16th century, 142
Puxley Hall, 122

Rathdrum, 82, 91
Rathedmond, 166
Rathfarnham, 70
Rathmullen, 146, 178
Raven's Glen, 92
Refeart Church, 90
Reformation, 200
Religious authoritarianism in Ireland, 23–5
Richard II, 84
Riders to the Sea (J. M. Synge), 138–9
Ringsend, 25–7, 34
Ringsend (Oliver St. John Gogarty), 27
Ringsend Park, 38
Rising of 1916, 18, 163, 172
Robertson, Daniel, 83
Robertstown, County Kildare, 46–8
Roquebrune, 176
Rosapenna, 189
Rosses, the, 194
Rosses Point, 162, 166, 167
Rosguill, 187–9
Roundwood, 80
Russborough, 82
Rutland Island, 194

St. Ailbe, 100
St. Audoen's Gate, Dublin, 57
St. Brendan, 109
St. Brigid, 102
St. Caimin, 105
St. Cavan, 139
St. Ciaran, 102, 106, 108
St. Colman, 102, 125–7
St. Colmcille, 171, 178, 185, 189
St. Diarmuid, 108
St. Enda, 139
St. Finbarr, 110
St. Finian, 171
St. Kevin, 84, 86, 88, 100, 124, 139
St. John's College, Kilkenny, 65
St. Patrick, 72, 96, 97–9, 200
  see also Patrick, controversy of the two saints
St. Patrick's cathedral, Dublin, 64–5

207